Cambridge Elements ≡

Elements in Organization Theory
edited by
Nelson Phillips
UC Santa Barbara
Royston Greenwood
University of Alberta

A CONNECTED WORLD

Social Networks and Organizations

Martin Kilduff
UCL School of Management
Lei Liu
University of Exeter Business School
Stefano Tasselli
*University of Exeter Business School and Erasmus
University Rotterdam*

CAMBRIDGE
UNIVERSITY PRESS

Shaftesbury Road, Cambridge CB2 8EA, United Kingdom

One Liberty Plaza, 20th Floor, New York, NY 10006, USA

477 Williamstown Road, Port Melbourne, VIC 3207, Australia

314–321, 3rd Floor, Plot 3, Splendor Forum, Jasola District Centre,
New Delhi – 110025, India

103 Penang Road, #05–06/07, Visioncrest Commercial, Singapore 238467

Cambridge University Press is part of Cambridge University Press & Assessment,
a department of the University of Cambridge.

We share the University's mission to contribute to society through the pursuit of
education, learning and research at the highest international levels of excellence.

www.cambridge.org
Information on this title: www.cambridge.org/9781009179492

DOI: 10.1017/9781009179508

First published 2023

A catalogue record for this publication is available from the British Library.

ISBN 978-1-009-17949-2 Paperback
ISSN 2397-947X (online)
ISSN 2514-3859 (print)

Cambridge University Press & Assessment has no responsibility for the persistence
or accuracy of URLs for external or third-party internet websites referred to in this
publication and does not guarantee that any content on such websites is, or will
remain, accurate or appropriate.

A Connected World

Social Networks and Organizations

Elements in Organization Theory

DOI: 10.1017/9781009179508
First published online: June 2023

Martin Kilduff
UCL School of Management

Lei Liu
University of Exeter Business School

Stefano Tasselli
University of Exeter Business School and Erasmus University Rotterdam

Author for correspondence: Martin Kilduff, m.kilduff@ucl.ac.uk

Abstract: This Element synthesizes the current state of research on organizational social networks from its early foundations to contemporary debates. It highlights the characteristics that make the social network perspective distinctive in the organizational research landscape, including its emphasis on structure and outcomes. It then covers the main theoretical developments and summarizes the research design questions that organizational researchers face when collecting and analyzing network data. Following this, it discusses current debates ranging from agency and structure to network volatility and personality. Finally, the Element envisages directions for future research on the role of brokerage for individuals and communities, network cognition, and the importance of past ties. Overall, the Element provides an innovative angle for understanding organizational social networks, engaging in empirical network research, and nurturing further theoretical development on the role of social interactions and connectedness in modern organizations.

Keywords: social network theory, social network methods, social network research, social network introduction, social network debates

ISBNs: 9781009179492 (PB), 9781009179508 (OC)
ISSNs: 2397-947X (online), 2514-3859 (print)

Contents

1 Introduction

Social network research provides an alternative research tradition to the focus within economics, sociology, and psychology on the demography, attitudes, and other attributes of individuals (e.g., Erickson, 1988). Network research moves beyond the exclusive study of individual attributes to focus on the social relations among a set of actors, including the connections among the actors as well as the gaps where connections are missing. When we use the word "actors," we refer to individual people or to other social units such as teams (e.g., Chung & Jackson, 2013) or organizations (e.g., Powell, Koput, & Smith-Doerr, 1996). Because of the focus on relationships, a bounded social network (one in which we know who all the actors are – e.g., an organizational department) is often represented as a graph in which points represent actors and lines represent connections (e.g., Mehra, Kilduff, & Brass, 1998), an approach pioneered in organizational behavior as far back as the Hawthorne studies (Roethlisberger & Dickson, 1939: 501–507). Bounded networks are characteristic features of intraorganizational network research relative to network research in other areas such as disease transmission where there is often a need for snowball sampling to establish the set of actors to be investigated (Biernacki & Waldorf, 1981). And organizational social network research, whether focused on inter-personal ties or organizational ties, tends to be less doctrinaire than sociological network research (e.g., Mayhew, 1980) in that it incorporates individual attributes such as gender or firm characteristics in order to explore synergies between actors and network structure (Kilduff & Brass, 2010).

Thus, the social network tradition derives intellectual capital from the pioneering social scientists, such as Fritz Heider, Kurt Lewin, and Jacob Moreno, who applied field-theoretic ideas (heralded by Einstein and others) to social interaction. In the work of Lewin (1936), there was a prescient emphasis on a dynamic and mathematical approach to individuals embedded within the field of social interaction. Moreno (1934) initiated the idea that an individual's position in a social network exposes the individual to social influence from others. Decisions made by individuals (such as decisions by delinquent girls to run away from their group home) can be understood not solely on the basis of individual predispositions but also on the basis of social network connections. Fritz Heider, the cotranslator of Lewin's (1936) book, went on to develop the parallels between mathematical representation and social interactions in his balance theory (Heider, 1946, 1958). From Heider's perspective, individuals who perceive their friendship relations as unrequited, or who perceive that their friends are not friends of each other, experience a strain toward balance – a tendency to correct these imbalanced relationships.

These advances by leading social scientists have influenced the development of social network research in terms of theory, topics, and methods. Lewin's emphasis on topology and a mathematical approach to social relations continues in the graph-theoretic basis of contemporary social network analysis (e.g., Wasserman & Faust, 1994). Moreno's deployment of social network diagrams ("sociograms") to depict and clarify patterns of interaction and influence has become a leading characteristic of social network research (Freeman, 2004). Balance theory has developed to include not just the cognitive perceptual field envisaged by Heider (1946) but also any set of influence or affect relationships that can be represented in graph-theoretic terms (Cartwright & Harary, 1956; Doreian & Mrvar, 2009). The application of social network ideas to complex organizations requires the use of high-speed computers. For macro research, a major boost was given by a review article detailing network ideas and applications (Tichy, Tushman, & Fombrun, 1979); for micro research, studies of interpersonal networks and outcomes set the agenda for future work (e.g., Brass, 1984).

In organizing this Element, we describe the distinctiveness of the social network approach, cover current theoretical developments, review research methods, discuss current debates, and look to future research trends. We draw mainly from the organizational literature, but also include key contributions from social science where the results are generalizable. Prior reviews provide succinct overviews of the social network approach (e.g., Brass, 2022), introductions for researchers (e.g., Prell, 2012), extensive coverage of methods (e.g., Scott & Carrington, 2011), and coverage of specialist topics such as brokerage (Stovel & Shaw, 2012) and dyadic ties (Rivera, Soderstrom, & Uzzi, 2010). The social network research area continues to accelerate in terms of new scholarship with recent reviews covering network brokerage (Kwon et al., 2020), gender and brokerage (Halevy & Kalish, 2021), network agency (Tasselli & Kilduff, 2021), the psychology of networks (Kilduff & Lee, 2020), and networks in international business (Cuypers et al., 2020). In the organizations area there are distinctive social network communities devoted to research within organizations (covering dyads, ego networks, and whole networks; Raider & Krackhardt, 2002) and between organizations (dealing with the firm as a network agent; Shipilov & Gawer, 2020). What holds this research together so that organizational researchers across topics and levels can communicate? Micro researchers tend to draw on the tradition of social psychology established by Heider and Lewin, whereas macro researchers tend to draw on theories of resource dependence (Pfeffer & Salancik, 1978) and embeddedness (Granovetter, 1985). But both communities invoke leading social network ideas (Kilduff & Brass, 2010) and employ common methods (as incorporated, for example, in such standard software packages as UCINET – Borgatti, Everett, & Freeman, 2002). Together these ideas and methods constitute a dynamic program of distinctive research.

2 Distinctiveness of Social Network Research

Argument and debate drive theory and research forward (Lakatos, 1970). One of the distinctive features of the social network field is the extent to which it hosts major debates concerning, for example whether to ignore attributes of individuals to focus on structural patterns (Mayhew, 1980), and whether social influence is better explained in terms of rivals in the social network striving to gain advantages over each other or in terms of connected colleagues providing help and advice to each other (Burt, 1987). In this sense, social network research is characterized by a distinctive set of evolving ideas rather than paradigmatic sterility (Kilduff, Tsai, & Hanke, 2006). Assumptions are challenged and leading ideas renewed through contention.

Thus, social network research exhibits a coherence at its core that allows it to embrace a variety of phenomena at different levels of analysis and across substantive areas. Researchers from across social science find in network research and analysis a common set of approaches and ideas. This commonality enables dialog across divides and generates innovative research endeavors.

What, then, are the distinctive ideas that drive the social network research program? The leading, interlocking ideas that drive the organizational social network program include the following (Kilduff & Brass, 2010): an emphasis on social relations as constitutive of organizational functioning; a recognition of the extent to which economic and other transactional exchanges are embedded within these social relations; an assumption that networks of relationships exhibit structural features such as clustering, gaps across clusters, and core/ periphery features; and an understanding that actors' positions in social networks provide advantages and disadvantages.

2.1 Emphasis on Social Relations

Certainly, the most basic emphasis in social network research is on the importance of social relationships (Freeman, 2004). Relationships can be conceptualized in terms of pipes through which resources, such as knowledge, flow; and in terms of prisms through which people's reputations are discerned: you are known by the people you are perceived to be connected to (Kilduff & Krackhardt, 1994; Podolny, 2001). Thus, while brokers can gain advantage from spanning across the gaps in social structure, they also have to be mindful of their reputations in the minds of those whose support they need for the pursuit of initiatives within their organizations (Podolny & Baron, 1997). Being seen to be connected to quite disparate groups can damage reputation (Zuckerman, 1999).

Relationships between organizational actors include positive ties such as friendship (Tasselli & Kilduff, 2018), advice (Krackhardt, 1990), and knowledge exchange (Tsai, 2001); but also include negative ties such as hindrance (Clarke, Richter, & Kilduff, 2021) and a preference for avoiding coworkers (Labianca, Brass, & Gray, 1998). Together these positive and negative ties constitute the social capital that is potentially available to an actor, defined as the goodwill inherent in the structure and content of social relations (Adler & Kwon, 2002: 18). As James Coleman (1988: 108) noted, ties such as friendship and acquaintanceship can be appropriated for other purposes such as getting a job (Fernandez, Castilla, & Moore, 2000; Granovetter, 1973) or facilitating team performance (Clarke et al., 2021). Ties to high status contacts can facilitate career advancement (Lin, 2001), whereas ties to leaders who are peripheral in their advice networks are detrimental to an actor's level of influence (Sparrowe & Liden, 2005). People who have many negative ties, relative to those who have few, are more likely to harm others and be the target of harm from others (Venkataramani & Dalal, 2007).

In the modern evolution of network research, the emphasis on social relationships has expanded to include relationship change (Rivera et al., 2010). Researchers have responded to the critiques concerning the neglect of network change (Emirbayer & Goodwin, 1994) with an increasing interest in network dynamics (Chen et al., 2022). Informal network connections are dynamic in the sense that social relationships shift and change over time as new technology is introduced in organizations (Barley, 1990; Sasovova et al., 2010), as new management is appointed (Burt & Ronchi, 1990), as new people are hired (Carley, 1991), and as people are promoted (Podolny & Baron, 1997). As networks of relationships change, our chances of becoming happy (Fowler & Christakis, 2008), depressed (Rosenquist, Fowler, & Christakis, 2011), or obese (Christakis & Fowler, 2007) also change.

In their everyday work lives, people have frequent opportunities to expand their networks by meeting new people but, it seems, relatively few people take advantage of social occasions to forge new relationships (Ingram & Morris, 2007). Patterns of relationships such as friendship stabilize relatively quickly within a bounded social system (such as a student living group – Newcomb, 1961) but under the surface there is likely to be considerable movement. Some actors form stable relations but others "dance between friends throughout the observation period" (Moody, McFarland, & Bender-deMoll, 2005: 1229).

The amount of churn individuals experience in their personal relations with others may derive in part from differences in underlying personality related to

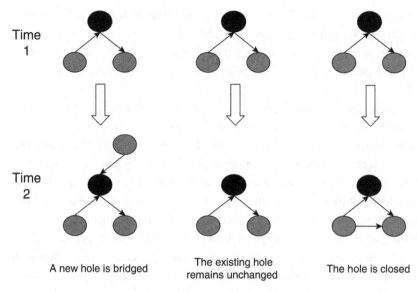

Time 1

Time 2

A new hole is bridged

The existing hole remains unchanged

The hole is closed

Figure 1 Brokerage opportunities change or remain the same over time.

the ease with which individuals manage impressions and social relationships (Sasovova et al., 2010). Similarly, individuals with a propensity to engage in brokerage (Burt, Jannotta, & Mahoney, 1998) are likely to experience considerable network change given that brokers trade across gaps in social structure (i.e., structural holes – Burt, 1992) and these gaps are subject to rapid decay in competitive organizations (Burt, 2002). Figure 1 illustrates some possibilities of how brokerage opportunities (structural holes) can expand, remain the same, or close over time. Relations between brokers and the unconnected parties to whom they offer a service tend to be fragile in part because of distrust of brokers who benefit from others' communication difficulties (Stovel, Golub, & Milgrom, 2011).

2.2 Embeddedness

An influential review declared that "embeddedness in social networks is increasingly seen as a root cause of human achievement, social stratification, and actor behavior" (Rivera et al., 2010: 91). Embeddedness refers to the overlap between social ties and economic ties; or the nesting of social ties within other ties (Kilduff & Brass, 2010). People are embedded to the extent that they show a preference for economic transactions with fellow network members (Granovetter, 1985). Embeddedness, including reliance on favored contacts for buying and selling, is important to the extent that markets are inefficient (Burt, 1992), but even in markets reputed to be highly efficient people tend to neglect interpersonal relationships at their peril (Abolafia & Kilduff, 1988; Baker, 1984). Social ties are forged, renewed, and extended through the network rather than through actors outside the network (Uzzi, 1996). Social connections between people that exist at one point in time tend to be repeated in the future (Rivera et al., 2010: 100).

People develop embeddedness when they overlay one type of connection with another type of connection – that is, when they develop multiplex ties in which more than one relationship is involved. Partners in law firms mitigate problems of status competition among their coworkers by developing multiplex ties of advice and friendship (Lazega & Pattison, 1999). Leaders of teams develop multiplex ties when they form both advice and friendship links with team members. These ties help leaders improve team performance when team social capital is otherwise impoverished (Clarke et al., 2021). People who are embedded (in terms of having large, dense, and high-quality relationships with colleagues in the workplace) tend to believe that the organization values their contributions and cares about their well-being (Hayton, Carnabuci, & Eisenberger, 2012). Individuals who are embedded in dense groups also tend to engage in interpersonal citizenship behaviors in organizations (Chung et al., 2011). But a pair of individuals tends to be less creative to the extent that their dyadic relationship is embedded within a dense network of common third parties – social pressure inhibits creative expression (Sosa, 2011).

Firm embeddedness refers to social ties among business owners within a community. This type of embeddedness both constrains and enables firm-level outcomes (Uzzi, 1997). On the plus side, social ties in a region create channels for contacts among managers and employees of firms, making it easier for firms to obtain knowledge about opportunities in foreign markets. Business relations embedded in social relations tend to affect outcomes in transitional economies relative to market economies (Luk et al., 2008). Managers rely more on relational ties as asset specificity and uncertainty increase (Zhou, Poppo, & Yang, 2008). But as ties become denser, there is an increasing likelihood that firms will interact only with local actors rather than pursuing foreign markets (Laursen, Masciarelli, & Prencipe, 2012). At the same time, potentially lucrative opportunities for entrepreneurs lie beyond embeddedness within their international communication networks (Ellis, 2011).

Embeddedness inhibits opportunism according to social capital theory (Granovetter, 1985). But the effects of embeddedness may be culturally contingent. A study of 192 international joint ventures found that, within collectivist versus individualist cultures, embeddedness, in the form of inter-party attachments and boundary-spanning ties, was a stronger inhibitor of opportunism (Luo, 2007). A related finding is that, among managers, affect and cognition-based trust are more intertwined in the collectivist culture of China relative to the individualist culture of the USA (Chua, Morris, & Ingram, 2009). What happens when West meets East? For partnerships between Western-based and Eastern-based firms, commitment to further exchanges predicts export performance and is itself driven by the reciprocal, reinforcing cycle of each partner's perception of the other's commitment (Styles, Patterson, & Ahmed, 2008).

Because organizations are dependent on each other for resources (Pfeffer & Salancik, 1978), they form alliances that help them survive in competitive markets. In knowledge-intensive industries such as biotechnology, firms embedded in collaborative alliances benefit from knowledge exchange that promotes learning and firm expansion (Powell et al., 1996). In these networked organizations (Powell, 1990), innovation happens in the interstices between firms rather than from internal research and development (Furnari, 2014). These cross-unit collaborations provide benefits to multinational organizations to the extent that they organize themselves as collaborative networks (Ghoshal & Bartlett, 1990).

2.3 Structural Patterning

Following on from the discussion of embeddedness, the third leading idea that distinguishes the social network research program concerns structural patterning – the notion that beneath the complexity of social relations are enduring patterns that can be discovered through analysis to show, for example, how actors cluster together or how networks are controlled by a few actors (e.g., Burt & Ronchi, 1990). Some social systems are organized in terms of a cohesive subgroup of core actors and a more peripheral set of actors loosely connected to the core. Where individuals are placed with respect to this core/periphery structure affects their outcomes, including their creativity (Cattani & Ferriani, 2008).

Other social systems can be understood as teams of actors forming and reforming over time. The success of these teams at any point in time depends not just on the accumulation of talent and motivation inherent in the team members (their human capital) but also on the extent of "connectivity and cleavage" (Wellman, 1988: 26) across the whole social system: the success of the team is dependent upon the social structure of the system within which the team operates (Uzzi & Spiro, 2005).

Structural analysis reveals the patterns of presence and absence in social networks that indicate clustering, connectivity, and centralization. Block model analysis (e.g., DiMaggio, 1986) and small-world analysis (e.g., Kilduff et al.,

2008) are configurational approaches that analyze patterns at the social network level rather than at the level of the individual (Dorogovtsev & Mendes, 2003), thereby permitting the study of the whole and the parts of social networks simultaneously (Wellman, 1988). Interest in the effects of structural patterning at different levels of analysis is growing. Individual attitudes, behaviors, and outcomes cannot be fully understood without considering the structuring of organizational contexts in which people are embedded (e.g., Tasselli & Sancino, 2023), whereas social network structuring and change in organizations cannot be fully understood without considering the psychology of purposive individuals (Tasselli, Kilduff, & Menges, 2015).

It is worthwhile emphasizing that the social structure of networks is by no means obvious to those who are members of such networks. Individuals are often mistaken concerning the patterns of relationships that include themselves and their colleagues (Landis et al., 2018). People tend to perceive themselves as more central in their friendship networks than they really are (Kumbasar, Romney, & Batchelder, 1994). They also forget casual attendees at meetings, tending to recall the meetings as attended by the habitual members of their social groups (Freeman, Romney, & Freeman, 1987). In one memorable example, a chief executive officer (CEO) of a troubled company that was subject to vandalism and bomb threats examined his firm's social network (gleaned from archival data by researchers) with bafflement. He had perceived his employees as "waves of turtles coming over the hill; hired as they made it to our door" (Burt, 1992: 1). He had not noticed the networks of kin, neighbors, and friends that constituted his personnel. The CEO had no clue about the deep cleavages that existed among his employees. Social network research has the possibility of emancipating people from default structural effects once structure and structural position are understood.

One of the most influential ideas in social network analysis relates to the uncovering of structural features by revealing the extent to which two individuals are structurally equivalent, that is, connected to the same other individuals (Lorrain & White, 1971). Through structural equivalence analysis, classes of equivalently positioned individuals can be detected (Boorman & White, 1976; White, Boorman, & Breiger, 1976). People who are structurally equivalent in terms of having similar relations to other people in advice and friendship networks tend to have similar views with respect to the organization and the support it offers to employees (Zagenczyk et al., 2010). Further, structurally equivalent employees tend to experience similar levels of emotional exhaustion at work even though their exhaustion levels are unrelated to those of their friends and supervisors (Zagenczyk, Powell, & Scott 2020).

2.4 Network Outcomes

The fourth leading idea of major importance to contemporary social network research is the emphasis on outcomes. The subfield of social capital research develops the theme that social network connections constrain and facilitate outcomes of importance to individuals and groups (Burt, 2000). Debates rage over the precise meaning of social capital (e.g., Borgatti, Jones, & Everett, 1998) given that it can be defined as "shared norms or values that promote social cooperation" (Fukuyama, 2002: 27) on the one hand and "investment in social relations with expected returns in the marketplace" (Lin, 2001: 19) on the other. At the individual level, social capital typically refers to the benefits that accrue from individual network connections (Tsai & Ghoshal, 1998). The value of social capital to an individual depends on the number of other people occupying the same social network position (Burt, 1997) – in this sense social capital is an arena for competition. The fewer the competitors who are structurally equivalent or in other ways occupy the individual's place in the social system, the greater the information and control benefits of brokerage across structural holes.

We live in an age in which people accumulate hundreds of friends and acquaintances through social media (Tong et al., 2008), while at the same time people report having fewer people in whom they can confide than was the case even a decade earlier (McPherson, Smith-Lovin, & Brashears, 2006). Social networks are important for survival – people who lack social and community ties are more likely to die than those with more extensive contacts (Berkman & Syme, 1979). Yet social and community engagement is declining outside the ranks of affluent young white people (Sander & Putnam, 2010). It might be thought that the massive increase in connectivity since the discovery that people could connect with complete strangers through about five intermediaries (Travers & Milgram, 1969) would drastically shrink the small world of interpersonal communication. But research suggests that it still takes between about five and seven intermediaries for email users to reach target persons by forwarding messages through acquaintances (Dodds, Muhamad, & Watts, 2003).

Social capital, irrespective of definitional debates, relates to outcomes of social network positions. Two of the major outcomes of importance to human beings are health and career progress. Health outcomes are clearly related to social capital. For example, longevity in cancer patients is greater for those with larger networks, and this is especially so for younger patients (Pinquart & Duberstein, 2010). People with more types of social ties (e.g., spouse, parent, friend, workmate, member of social group) are less susceptible to catching the common cold (Cohen et al., 1997). Social networks can affect health through a variety of mechanisms including social support, social influence, access to resources, social involvement, and person-to-person contagion (see Smith & Christakis, 2008 for a review). However, despite the strong and reliable association between the diversity of social networks and longevity and disease risk, there is still little understanding of how interventions might influence key components of the network to improve physical health (Cohen & Janicki-Deverts, 2009). Complicating matters is evidence that the relationship between health and networks is bidirectional: health behavior also affects social networks. For example, adolescents select friends whose smoking levels are similar to their own. Rather dismayingly, the data show that adolescent smokers are more likely than nonsmokers to be named as friends (Schaefer, Haas, & Bishop, 2012).

Social capital relates not just to health but also to important career issues. Bankers who have strong ties to colleagues from whom they receive important information concerning deals but whose colleagues are only sparsely connected among themselves receive high bonuses (Mizruchi, Stearns, & Fleischer, 2011). People who can potentially act as go-betweens for colleagues who are themselves not connected tend to have higher performance (e.g., Mehra, Kilduff, & Brass, 2001). As a major review of the network structure of social capital makes clear, people who develop large, sparse, nonhierarchical networks that are rich in opportunities to broker connections across structural holes tend to be more creative; they tend also to receive more positive job evaluations, early promotions, and higher earnings (Burt, 2000). In contrast, people whose work-related networks feature densely-connected cliques of friends tend to experience substandard performance in organizations and substandard rewards.

The contrast between brokerage and closure networks is shown in Figure 2, which illustrates a situation in which Jen has taken over Robin's job. Robin had a relatively closed network, spanning across only one structural hole between Groups 1 and 2. Jen restructured the network and expanded the social capital associated with the job by adding two new clusters of people in addition to the

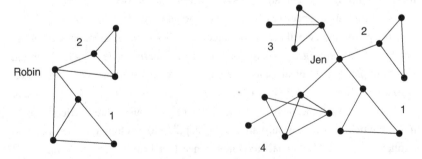

Figure 2 Managing structural holes between groups.

two clusters reached by Robin's network. Jen, like Robin, only had to manage four ties, but in the reconfigured network Jen bridges across six structural holes between the four groups. Thus, Jen's network is both more efficient and more effective than Robin's.

Despite the importance of maintaining a diverse network that provides information and control benefits, the individual is also well advised to build cohesive ties with the "buy-in" network – that small group of people in the organization who have control over the individual's fate. A lack of cohesiveness among those with fate control impedes the individual's advancement, whereas the individual's average closeness to those with fate control has a strong positive effect on mobility (Podolny & Baron, 1997). Cohesion is also valuable in teams. Meta-analysis shows that the higher the density of ties within a team, the more the team members commit to staying together and achieving their goals (Balkundi & Harrison, 2006). But ties external to the team are also crucial. To the extent that the team leader is connected to popular team leaders within the overall organization, the team tends to be more productive (Mehra et al., 2006). More generally, teams that have numerous connections beyond the team to other actors that are themselves disconnected from each other (i.e., nonredundant connections), will have access to a broader diversity of perspectives, skills, and resources, and therefore can be expected to perform well (Burt, 2000: 398).

These leading ideas (summarized in Table 1) – the emphasis on social relations, embeddedness, structure, and network outcomes – will interweave throughout this Element (Kilduff & Brass, 2010).

3 Theoretical Developments

Social network theory tends to develop through a series of juxtaposed perspectives. For example, the structural equivalence approach (emphasizing competition between rivals for the same network position - White et al., 1976) has been pitted (Burt, 1987) against the cohesion approach (emphasizing cooperation among friends and acquaintances – Coleman, Katz, & Menzel, 1966). The weak-tie approach (Granovetter, 1973) has been challenged by the strong-tie perspective (Krackhardt, 1992). And the structural-hole perspective has been contrasted with closure (Burt, 2005). The first debate (between structural equivalence and cohesion) has generated a fascinating body of research concerning conflicting empirical claims (see Kilduff & Oh, 2006 for a review). Recent research shows that both cohesion and structural equivalence help explain how teenagers target their aggression as they strive for social status (Faris, Felmlee, & McMillan 2020). This research advances the argument, previously made by Burt (1987), that structurally equivalent alters represent rivals for the individual's social position, an argument that has the potential to

Table 1 Leading social network ideas.

	Key citations
Social relationships: Network research assumes the importance of relations that connect and divide individuals, groups, organizations, and other actors.	Freeman, 2004; Tichy et al., 1979
Embeddedness refers to actors' preference for transacting with social network members; it also refers to the preference for forging, extending, and renewing social ties within and through the existing social network.	Granovetter, 1985; Uzzi, 1996
Structural patterning: Network research examines patterns of clustering, connectivity, centralization, small-worldness, and other structural features of social networks.	Wellman & Berkowitz, 1988; White et al., 1976
Social network outcomes: Network connections constitute the social capital that facilitates outcomes of importance to individuals and groups.	Burt, 1992; Nahapiet & Ghoshal, 1998

be developed theoretically and empirically given the upsurge in interest in rivalry (e.g., Kilduff, 2019).

We will concentrate on the second and third contrasts mentioned at the start of this section because these approaches dominate the theoretical framings in our literature; and resemble each other in that a bridging perspective (weak ties or structural holes) contrasts with a bonding perspective (strong ties or closure).

Indeed, in social network theory and research there are two distinctive traditions, one emphasizing the microdynamics of strategic engagement among people who know each other well and who work in close proximity, the other emphasizing the network structures and distant influences that inhibit and facilitate the outcomes not just of individuals but also of communities. These two traditions that continue to inspire contemporary research derive from foundational works in sociology published in the late 19th and early 20th centuries (for translations, see Durkheim, 1951, and Simmel, 1950). We summarize a brief history of these perspectives and discuss the two juxtaposed perspectives that spring from this theoretical tension: structural-hole theory and weak-tie theory.

The strategic engagement perspective is exemplified in Georg Simmel's (1950, originally published 1908) analysis of *tertius gaudens* – the third who benefits from the conflict or disunity of the other two members of a three-person group. According to Simmel, "the non-partisan may . . . make the interaction that takes place between the parties and between himself and them, a means for his own purpose" (Simmel, 1950: 154). This strategic engagement approach can be traced forward through the work of Goffman (1969) concerning the discovery and transmission of information between individuals in face-to-face interaction; it is continued in current game-theoretic treatments of how individuals can extract profit from social network brokerage (e.g., Goyal, 2007). In contemporary social network research, it is the structural-hole perspective (Burt, 1980, 1992, 2005, 2010) that most clearly exemplifies this emphasis on *tertius gaudens* strategic engagement.

Quite different in its emphasis is the community structure tradition that can be traced back at least as far as Émile Durkheim, who analyzed the ways in which individuals' most personal decisions were explicable by their location in social and societal contexts (e.g., Durkheim, 1951, first published in 1897). Rather than being free to manipulate outcomes in the ways that strategic engagement perspectives suggest, the people in Durkheim's account are portrayed as fortunate or unlucky recipients of social and cultural influence. As more recent research shows, the nature of the relationship between two people reflects the structure of relations around each person in his or her own distinctive network. How two people relate to each other is not entirely within their control (Bott, 1955). Further, social encounters themselves reflect the numerical properties of the groups to which people belong rather than just people's own volitions (Blau, 1977). As one empirical investigation demonstrated, "the greater the heterogeneity the greater are the chances that any fortuitous encounter involves persons of different groups" (Blau, Blum, & Schwartz, 1982: 47). Economic migrants, who might be thought to be suffering from anomie, benefit from chains of influence involving coethnics within local and worldwide communities (Wellman, 1979). Further, the structure of community ties is itself affected by individuals' private decisions in ways that individuals themselves are unaware of, as noted by a theorist commonly associated with the "closure" tradition of social networks. An example given by Coleman is of a family deciding to move away from a community because of a job opportunity elsewhere, a decision that severs relations with those left behind thereby potentially weakening norms and sanctions that aid parents and schools in socializing children (Coleman, 1990: 316). As this example illustrates, community members can be affected by others' decisions over which they have no control.

The community structure theme was taken up by Stanley Milgram (1967) with his emphasis on connectivity in small worlds – defined as social networks that exhibit two features rarely found together, namely, clustering and connectivity (Kilduff et al., 2008). Small-world research shows (a) that the success of a team's artistic production depends on the overall state of community small-worldness (Uzzi & Spiro, 2005); and (b) that small-world structures derive from chance rather than strategic action by dominant forces (Baum, Shipilov, & Rowley, 2003).

This Durkheimian emphasis continues in research examining how connections far removed from the individual affect the individual's loneliness (Cacioppo, Fowler, & Christakis, 2009) and happiness (Fowler & Christakis, 2008). These outcomes are, in part, therefore, the results of individuals' placements in community structures that they cannot hope to control. This community structure perspective is prominent in the theoretical work associated with Mark Granovetter in two foundational research articles concerned with the strength of weak ties (Granovetter, 1973) and the extent to which economic relations are embedded in social relations (Granovetter, 1985).

Despite the clear difference between these two research traditions, one emphasizing the strategic manipulation of close network relations (e.g., Burt, 1992) and the other emphasizing the embeddedness of individuals within communities (e.g., Granovetter, 1973, 1985), in theory and research concerning workplace interactions, this difference has proved elusive in recent research because of the overlap between weak-tie and structural-hole approaches.

One paper on the strength of weak ties (Granovetter, 1973) has claims to be the most influential ever published in sociology (Fernandez, 2021). It posits that, relative to strong ties such as friendship, weak ties, measured in terms of time spent in a relationship and the depth of the relationship (Marsden & Campbell, 1984), lead to more employment opportunities, career outcomes, creativity, and performance (Rajkumar et al., 2022). The basic idea is that weak ties bring us into contact with people outside our overlapping circles of friends and therefore expose us to useful information that we would not otherwise glean.

Structural-hole theory builds on the weak-tie approach but questions the importance of tie strength (Burt, 1992). What is of importance from a structural-hole perspective is not the quality of any particular tie but rather the way different, disconnected parts of networks are bridged by individuals for their own advantage. Thus, the benefits to the individual from bridging ties are decoupled from the average strength of those ties (Podolny, 2001: 34). But this still leaves weak-tie and structural-hole ideas as distinctively different core principles of how social networks relate to economic outcomes (Granovetter, 2005: 35).

3.1 Development of Structural-Hole and Weak-Tie Theory

Structural-hole theory, like every generative social theory, has shown vigorous evolution since its earlier articulation in terms of the advantage of disconnected contacts (Burt, 1980). In the earlier articulation the emphasis (borrowing from Simmel, 1950) was on the extent to which actors achieved autonomy by occupying positions that had many conflicting group affiliations. Prefiguring the later emphasis on how diverse contacts reduced constraint, the autonomy argument emphasized how "the pattern of relations defining the network position 'frees' occupants of the position from constraint by others" (Burt, 1980: 922). In the later development of this argument as it affected interpersonal relations, the emphasis changed from structural positions (occupied by structurally equivalent actors – Burt, 1980) to individual persons, and from freedom from constraint to the contrast between constraint on the one hand and control on the other (Burt, 1992). More recently, the micro-macro dynamic has, following empirical results (Burt, 2007), encompassed ego within the restricted focus of ego's direct contacts, thereby eschewing implications concerning the much wider community (Burt, 2010).

There is also a developing emphasis on differences among individuals in terms of their ability to recognize and take advantage of structural-hole positioning (Burt, 2005: 23). People display consistency across situations in whether they build closed or open social networks, and this consistency is suggestive of individual agency in network construction. Achievement is determined by the individual's role experience and their role-specific network (Burt, 2012). Note, however, that despite this developing emphasis on individualism, structural-hole theory envisages companies benefiting from the activities of individuals who span across structural holes in the social fabric of the organization. These network brokers are "highly mobile relative to the bureaucracy" in providing faster and better solutions (Burt, 1992: 116).

Weak ties are those characterized by infrequent interaction, short history, and limited (emotional) closeness (Granovetter, 1973). Weak ties are "ideal vehicles for access and exposure to very different thought worlds – perspectives and approaches that are not only new to the actor but … fundamentally different from each other" (Baer, 2010: 592–593). In the weak-tie approach (Granovetter, 1973, 1983), the emphasis is on bridging to distant clusters rather than on cementing relations with close friends or kin. To break out of the comforting entrapment of one's close circle of friends and family requires contact with a quite different social circle, contact that is unlikely to derive from a strong tie given that those with whom we maintain strong ties are likely to know the same people we do. It is through weak ties (such as infrequent encounters between two people in the supply chain) that novel opportunities and resources are likely to become available. A key hypothesis in weak-tie theory is: "the stronger the tie between A and B, the larger the proportion of individuals in S to whom they will *both* be tied" (Granovetter, 1973: 1362). This is a theory about how the relationship between two people can affect embeddedness in larger community structures and how community structure can affect the fates both of individuals and of the clusters to which they belong. The micro-macro dynamic in weak-tie theory encompasses not just the individual, the dyad, and the local cluster to which individuals and dyads belong (as in structural-hole theory); it also incorporates the ways in which individuals, dyads, and clusters reciprocally relate to much larger community structures.

Structural-hole theory, among its many other contributions, is valuable for pointing out that bridging ties – whether strong or weak – are key to understanding how individuals achieve advantage in situations in which information represents a scarce resource (Burt, 2005: 18). Structural-hole theory is similar to and builds on weak-tie theory's discussion of the benefits of diverse information. One of the valuable aspects of Burt's 1992 explication is the differentiation of these benefits into those of access, timing, and referrals (Burt, 1992: 13–15), benefits encompassed by both weak-tie theory and structural-hole theory. Briefly, in terms of access, some people are better positioned than others to use their networks to screen important news and opportunities. Similarly, some people have personal contacts who provide them with information before others receive it. And in terms of referrals, some people have personal contacts who make sure their names are mentioned at the right time in the right place so that opportunities are made available. All of this is compatible with weak-tie theory, although the emphasis in structural-hole theory is on people "who can speak to your virtues" (Burt, 1992: 15), prefiguring the more recent emphasis on benefits that flow from the immediate set of contacts around the individual rather than from secondary and more distant contacts. Thus, according to a recent treatment of structural-hole theory, accessing structural holes beyond the ego network provides little benefit (Burt, 2007, 2010). This more recent development of structural-hole theory differentiates it from weak-tie theory's emphasis on benefits flowing from afar.

3.2 Juxtaposing Structural-Hole and Weak-Tie Approaches

Differences between the two theories relate to the emphases on control, tie strength, traversing social distance, accuracy of social perception, and micro–macro links.

3.2.1 Control

Given the emphasis on weak ties as bridging social distance, weak-tie theory highlights the extent to which the social network outcomes of individual workers are typically beyond their control: "The personal experience of individuals is closely bound up with large-scale aspects of social structure, well beyond the purview or control of particular individuals" (Granovetter, 1973: 1377). How important are the control benefits to the distinctiveness of structural-hole theory? The theory emphasizes that "the weak tie argument obscures the control benefits of structural holes" and states that "control benefits augment and in some ways are more important than the information benefits of structural holes" (Burt, 1992: 28). It is not just that the broker pursues a strategy of extracting benefits from the existing structure of the network (spanning across existing structural holes); rather, the broker also benefits from a strategy of actively intervening to manipulate situations: "control benefits require an active hand in the distribution of information . . . . The *tertius* plays conflicting demands and preferences against one another and builds value from their disunion" (Burt, 1992: 34). The activities of the broker extend to changing the network to undermine others in pursuit of gain, as this quotation makes clear concerning strategies for dealing with a "truculent" boss: "the player could expand the network to include someone who could undermine the boss's control, perhaps a peer or superior to the boss who could be played against the truculent boss in a *tertius* strategy" (Burt, 1992: 67–68).

More generally, in structural-hole theory, brokers manufacture holes, withdraw from relationships that are constraining, and bring in new contacts to neutralize or disadvantage those that are constraining (Burt, 1992: 230–238). This emphasis on the strategic creation of structural holes has been carried forward by others who use structural-hole theory to emphasize "a more competitive orientation" in which actors "attempt to segregate information, selectively building – as well as undermining – trust . . . to increase others' dependence on them and their power in the network" (Baum et al., 2003: 704). Thus, in contrast to weak-tie theory, the *tertius gaudens* strategy involves a broker not just passively receiving benefits because of his or her structural position in the network but also strategically controlling the flow of information among two or more unconnected contacts, manufacturing division among alters, and exploiting the conditions of uncertainty, on occasion, to undermine others for personal advantage. Recent theory identifies a *tertius separans* strategic orientation by individual actors toward keeping alters separate for the benefit of ego (Burt, 2021).

Thus, a major distinction between the weak-tie approach and the structural-hole approach concerns the extent to which the individual is in control of brokerage. In the weak-tie approach, given unclear boundaries, lack of awareness of social structure, and the general flux of social interaction characteristic of everyday life in a boundaryless world (Direnzo & Greenhaus, 2011), the individual benefits to a greater or lesser extent from chance encounters that have the possibility of connecting the individual to distant social worlds from which new knowledge and creative ideas are likely to flow. In the structural-hole approach, given its emphasis on local context within which the individual is centrally located, the emphasis is on the focal individual controlling information flow between alters. In the weak-tie approach, given the emphasis on bridging to distant others, there is the possibility that low-status actors will benefit from connections to those of higher status. In the structural-hole approach, there is an emphasis on ways in which the absence of connections among alters can be exploited by social network brokers for personal gain even as the efficiency of organizational processes are enhanced through their coordination efforts.

3.2.2 Strength of Tie

Structural-hole theory also differentiates itself from weak-tie theory through an emphasis on the strength of ties between ego and alters that is necessary to ensure control. From a weak-tie perspective, new pieces of information – such as news about job openings, market opportunities, and resource constraints – arrive through chance meetings, such as with prior colleagues and acquaintances. As Granovetter (1973: 1372) pointed out: "It is remarkable that people receive crucial information from individuals whose very existence they have forgotten." (For information on conceptualization and measurement of tie strength, see Marsden & Campbell, 2012.)

The structural-hole approach frequently (but not universally) incorporates a sophisticated measure of tie strength in the constraint measure. This feature of the constraint measure is useful in cases where researchers follow Burt (1992) in assessing structural-hole spanning across both positive relationships and negative relationships, encompassing, for example, both "the three people you have been with most often for informal social activities" and the people who have "made it the most difficult for you to carry out your job responsibilities" (Burt, 1992: 123). Empirically, the constraint measure is based upon core relations of the individual, including people who are sources of frequent socializing, advice-seeking, and buy-in (Burt, 1992, 2002, 2004), corresponding to Burt's (2010: 45) theoretical focus on brokerage opportunities among "ego's close, personal relationships." Different from weak-tie theory is the emphasis (embodied in the constraint measure) on both core contacts and the extent to which individuals invest network time and energy in a single core contact or a concentrated group of interconnected core contacts. This insightful emphasis on how the individual's network can be controlled by an alter goes beyond weak-tie theory's emphasis on closure through transitive triads.

It is important to note that structural-hole theory recognizes the value of strong connections between the focal individual and alters on the one hand (to ensure control) and the inconsequential nature of weak ties among alters on the other. For brokers who wish to access and control information, strong ties are emphasized, as in this explanation: "A structural hole indicates that the people on either side of the hole circulate in different flows of information. A manager who spans the structural hole, by having strong relations with contacts on both sides of the hole, has access to both information flows" (Burt, 1997: 341).

Thus, strong ties facilitate ego's access and control. And weak ties among the alters do little to diminish this access and control. According to expositions of structural-hole theory in several places, structural holes are not necessarily completely free of bridging connections; rather, they are free of *strong connections*: "the hole is the relatively weak connection between [clusters]" (Burt, 1997: 341). Similarly, in another exposition of structural-hole theory, structural holes are defined as existing when social space is spanned by weak ties: "It is the weak connections (structural holes) between Robert's contacts that provide his expanded social capital" (Burt, 1998: 9). A weak tie across alters, therefore, is treated in these explanations of the theory as no connection at all. Note, however, that weak ties from ego to alters, as in weak-tie theory, are recognized as weak-tie bridges (e.g., Burt, 2005: 24) whose benefits may be worthy of further research (Burt, 2002: 339). There is, therefore, some ambiguity concerning strength of tie in relation to structural-hole theory, despite the clear formalization of the theory in a constraint measure that includes strength of tie as one of its components (Burt, 1992: 50–81). This ambiguity is perhaps necessary given the wide-ranging nature and the generative power of structural-hole theory.

3.2.3 Traversing Social Distance

A third major difference from weak-tie theory is the increasing emphasis within structural-hole theory placed on brokerage opportunities across an individual's immediate local social network, that is, across the structure of relations among "ego's close, personal relationships" (Burt, 2010: 45). Although early versions of structural-hole theory contemplated benefits deriving from structural holes among contacts of contacts (Burt, 1992), the emphasis of the theory has moved progressively toward a micro-focus on benefits deriving only from gaps among the individual's direct contacts in the workplace (Burt, 2007). Invoking the idea of "sticky information" (von Hippel, 1994), structural-hole theory posits that when information is moved beyond an individual's local network, the information can lose its meaning and become misunderstood or miscommunicated (Burt, 2010). Due to the characteristics of the information (e.g., tacit nature) or the characteristics of the people processing the information (e.g., lack of shared understanding), information can be sticky to move. Brokerage is argued to be less successful once information has to be moved beyond the immediate circle of contacts in the workplace around the individual because an individual is less likely to share vocabularies, taken-for-granted understandings, or routines with socially distant contacts. Secondhand brokerage – movement of information across the disconnected contacts of alters – has a negligible association with individual performance over and above the association of direct brokerage (Burt, 2007). This emphasis on direct brokerage between the focal individual and his or her alters is different from the emphasis within weak-tie theory.

From the weak-tie perspective, a bridge between two individuals does not have to be the only social path connecting them. What is important is that the bridge functions as a vital link on the shortest path, contributing significantly to the ease with which people in distant parts of the network reach each other. An important insight of weak-tie theory is that "long" spanning ties (i.e., ties that span between individuals far removed from each other in the social network) tend to be weak (Centola & Macy, 2007) because strong ties, relative to weak ties, are at a higher risk of social closure. Presciently, weak-tie theory in its earliest formulation (Granovetter, 1973) linked Milgram's (1967) work on small worlds to weak ties, noting how distant individuals are more likely to be reached through acquaintances than friends – an insight replicated in more recent small-world research (e.g., Dodds et al., 2003). In small-world terminology, "long-range shortcuts" (Watts, 1999: 511) tend to be weak ties, connecting what would otherwise be distant parts of a network involving long path-lengths. It is this short access across social distance that gives rise to network advantage in terms of receiving distant information or influence (e.g., Lin, Ensel, & Vaughn, 1981; Montgomery, 1992; Yakubovich, 2005).

Whereas weak-tie theory zooms out to emphasize distant connectivity beyond ego's immediate cluster of close relationships, structural-hole theory zooms in to focus on the local social network surrounding ego. Emphasizing control benefits through brokerage, a bridge in structural-hole theory is about spanning the missing relation between two alters rather than spanning social distance. The theme of planned, active maneuvering and negotiation to control the flow of resources across unconnected alters for personal benefits is strong in the structural-hole approach (Burt, 1992; Fernandez & Gould, 1994), and stands out against the role of serendipity in the weak-tie approach. Returns to strategic brokerage hinge on the ego-alter sharing of "concerns, unspoken assumptions and vocabularies" (Burt, 2010: 46) – understandings more likely to be shared among direct close alters than socially distant alters; as such, secondhand brokerage fails to yield rewards since the lack of understandings inhibits the movement of information across socially distant alters (Burt, 2007). Thus, weak ties connect the individual (and individual clusters of people) to distant social sources of distinctive information (Centola & Macy, 2007), whereas in the structural-hole account it is in the local network surrounding the individual employee that opportunity is there to be exploited (Buskens & van de Rijt, 2008).

3.2.4 Acuity

Fourth, structural-hole theory differs from weak-tie theory by attributing to brokers a "vision advantage" (Burt, 2004: 354) such that brokers "are able to see early, see more broadly, and translate information across groups." Brokers, because of their network position, have greater acuity in network perception. Empirical research on network perception has shown that individuals who report experience spanning across structural holes are, indeed, more accurate in perceiving and remembering gaps in networks (Janicik & Larrick, 2005). The weak-tie approach, by contrast, assumes no such advantage. Rather, individuals tend to be embedded in their local clusters to the extent that they are unable to perceive community structures of relevance to their aspirations and futures (Granovetter, 1973, 2005). It is precisely because of this embeddedness that weak ties are so valuable in potentially opening channels to hitherto unknown groups and sources of information and ideas.

Relative to the structural-hole approach, therefore, there is less emphasis in weak-tie theory on individuals accurately perceiving the structure of social networks in which they are embedded, an accuracy that would seem to be required for the manipulation and control of networks in the structural-hole approach.

3.3 Micro–Macro Links: From Juxtaposing to Integrating the Two Theories

If advantage in the structural-hole approach derives from brokerage in ego's immediate network of alters, then it is not surprising that its theoretical lens centers on local networks and local outcomes (Burt, 2010). Central to weak-tie theory, however, is the exploration of how local, micro relationships lead to global, macro patterns (Granovetter, 1973). If weak ties are less prone to triadic closure and, thus, span greater social distance, they are more likely to serve as the crucial informal connections helping to hold together separated business units within an overall collectivity. Formation or deletion of weak ties at the local level can therefore have significant consequences on structural integration or fragmentation at the global level. Local processes such as formation of weak ties, for instance, have been characterized as contributing to the formation of a small world at the global level, where highly clustered groups are connected by short path-lengths (Dodds et al., 2003; Robins, Pattison, & Woolcock, 2005). Thus, a powerful contribution of weak-tie theory is in explaining how local network changes shape global network connectivity, a point less emphasized in structural-hole theory.

Weak-tie theory has always had a double focus: a micro-focus on the strength of the direct tie between the individual and that individual's contacts within and beyond the workplace, as well as a more macro focus on the structure of ties across the whole community of interests that constitutes the modern firm. It is this double focus that gives the theory much of its distinctiveness – it is one of the few social theories that compellingly relates the activities of individuals to the fates of communities. Extending the theory to the situation of people within an organizational unit who develop strong ties of cohesion among themselves, even in the face of pressures toward globalization, we can say that this internal bonding restricts the opportunities available to each employee of that unit. Relatedly, if each employee exclusively restricts him- or herself to strong-tie attachments, this reduces the resilience of the business unit in the face of unexpected jolts because the business unit will not have allies elsewhere in the wider organization or in the value chain (Krackhardt & Stern, 1988).

The causal mechanisms in weak-tie theory are different from those posited in structural-hole theory. At the individual level, it is access to socially distant resources that provides the individual with advantage in the weak-tie account. At the community level, it is integration through weak ties across fragmented social groups that provides resilience in the face of threats to the social order and persistence of the community. But this is quite different from the active broker-age posited by structural-hole theory that anticipates the individual controlling the flow of information between disconnected alters.

In sharpening the distinctions between the weak-tie approach and the structural-hole perspective, we can ask: how do the classic themes of strategy and serendipity play out in the pursuit of advantage? What, for example, would a strategic approach involve from a weak-tie perspective? One of the advantages of weak ties is that they require lower time commitments relative to strong ties, and, thus, increase the occurrence of serendipitous encounters (for which there is more time, and concerning which there is more likelihood). Thus, one possible weak-tie strategy would be for individuals to develop many weak ties, not knowing which ones might or might not connect to socially distant sources of diverse information and opportunity. This "real options" approach helps hedge against uncertainty concerning how the network and the competitive landscape evolve (Gulati, Nohria, & Zaheer, 2000).

We have already discussed the emphasis within the structural-hole approach on the strategic manipulation of ties, but we can say a little more in the way of clarifying theory. There is a consistent emphasis within structural-hole theory on brokers as active agents striving for advantage, as exemplified in this quotation: "[P]eople with networks rich in structural holes are the people who know about, have a hand in, and exercise control over, more rewarding opportunities" (Burt, 2005: 18). But structural-hole theory also incorporates the likelihood that individuals in positions that span across structural holes are at risk of good ideas and rewarding opportunities even if they fail to recognize these ideas and opportunities or choose to pursue them. The emphasis on strategic agency does not rule out the possibility that agency can benefit from serendipity. Given the considerable churn in even the close ties of organizational members (Sasovova et al., 2010), this "pulsing swirl of mixed, conflicting demands" (Burt, 1992: 33) requires on the part of network brokers an active manufacturing of bridges: "Where structural holes do not exist, they can be manufactured, or their absence can be neutralized" (Burt, 1992: 230).

Further, structural-hole theory advocates the principle of divide and rule, building on the work of Merton (1968: 393–394) and Simmel (1950: 185–186). From this perspective, the broker manufactures competition between alters to establish control by creating conflict where it otherwise might not exist: "Make simultaneous, contradictory demands explicit to the people posing them, and ask them to resolve their – now explicit – conflict. Even where it doesn't exist, competition can be produced by defining issues such that contact demands become contradictory and must be resolved before you can meet their requests .... [I]f the strategy is successful, the pressure on you is alleviated and is replaced with an element of control over the negotiation" (Burt, 1992: 31). The promotion of latent conflict and competition and the guarding against possible collaboration by alters (Burt, 1992: 30–32) differentiate the structural-hole approach from the emphasis on serendipity characteristic of weak-tie theory.

The architecture of the ideal organizational network suggested by both weak-tie theory (Granovetter, 1973) and structural-hole theory (Burt, 2005: 12–13) resembles a small world of cohesive clusters (that represent distinctive sources of knowledge, opportunity, and resources) connected by bridges across which knowledge, opportunity, and resources can flow. However, because weak-tie theory emphasizes information from afar, whereas structural-hole theory emphasizes local control of disconnected alters, there may be different implications depending upon which theoretical lens is adopted. To the extent that strong ties are the focus of structural-hole theory, the implications of weak ties may be missed. Weak ties are not means through which ego controls alters, but they may well be pipes through which resources temporary or consistent flow (Hansen, 1999). They may be present but unseen in networks exhibiting apparent structural holes, thereby limiting the information benefits to ego and reducing the extent to which control is possible.

An important difference between the two approaches, from a configuration aspect, is that the weak-tie approach posits the possibility of information and resources flowing from afar across unclear boundaries, whereas the structural-hole approach seems to require a well-bounded social network within which the network broker can operate. Thus, structural-hole theory has found a natural home in the analysis of social networks within bounded business units (Burt, 2007), whereas weak-tie theory has been applied to situations such as labor markets where the boundaries of opportunity from the individual's perspective are unclear (e.g., Montgomery, 1992). In the boundaryless modern workplace, it may be possible for an updated weak-tie theory to help us understand how careers develop and resources flow as vertical, horizontal, external, and geographical organizational boundaries are minimized, and as people pursue advantage both within and across current employers (Arthur & Rousseau, 1996).

In conclusion, both weak-tie and structural-hole approaches are relevant and generative theoretical frameworks for research on social networks. For weak-tie theory, a recent experiment (Rajkumar et al., 2022) on 20 million people over a 5-year period, during which 600,000 new jobs were created, showed support for the causal claim that weak ties increase job transmission, but suggested that, after a point, there were diminishing marginal returns to tie weakness. And weak ties were particularly generative of job opportunities in digital industries. Structural-hole theory contributes to a burgeoning research program on different types of brokerage (e.g., Nicolaou & Kilduff, 2022), and the antecedents, mechanisms, and outcomes of brokerage positions and processes (Kwon et al., 2020).

4 Social Network Research Methods

4.1 What Kind of Research Do You Propose?

Because the study of organizational social networks is a fertile research arena, in which new studies contribute to the sophistication of existing theoretical

Epistemology

Social network research gets closer and closer to the truth?

		Yes	No
Ontology Social network theories represent reality?	Yes	*Structural Realism* Uncover basic structural properties of networks (e.g., Lorrain & White, 1971).	*Paradigm Extending* Work within a dominant social network theory to address anomalies and puzzles (e.g., Burt, 2007).
	No	*Foundationalism* Analyze big data to uncover new social network processes (e.g., Dorogovtsev & Mendes, 2003).	*Instrumentalism* Address an empirical problem using social network tools (e.g., Cross, Borgatti, & Parker, 2002).

Figure 3 Four different approaches to social network research.

approaches in answering an evolving set of questions, understanding the basic assumptions of your research approach is important. As with any research initiative, a social network research endeavor can proceed according to different underlying assumptions. Being clear about the kind of research you are engaged in can facilitate progress and reduce misunderstanding among members of the research team. There are four basic types of research endeavor, organized according to questions concerning epistemology and ontology. The four approaches are illustrated in Figure 3, which poses two questions as you begin your research journey: Are you trying to move closer to the truth about the world? And do you believe that the theory you are working with represents reality? In this section, we present the rationale behind the four approaches. Then, we discuss basic methodological choices that researchers interested in social network analysis must face.

4.1.1 Structural Realism

First, if you are intent on uncovering basic truths about social network structure, then you are engaged in a structural realist pursuit and your answers to the two questions are in the affirmative, as Figure 3 shows. Structural realism is exemplified in the mathematical social network research of Lorrain and White (1971) who discovered how complex crisscrossing patterns of relationships can reduce to simpler subsets to reveal unexpected similarities between people. Their discovery of structural equivalence provided the basis for block-model analysis that reduces relatively incoherent social networks into more readily interpretable patterns. For example, the patterns of intermarriage and economic relationship among Florence's ninety-two-family ruling elite during the fifteenth century can be simplified through block-modeling to reveal how the Medici family, and in particular Cosmo de' Medici, exploited network disjunctures to increase family power and control (Padgett & Ansell, 1993). A much different use of the structural equivalence idea exemplified the snowball effect – the process by which employee turnover occurs in clusters of employees who see themselves as occupying similar informal roles in the workplace communication network (Krackhardt & Porter, 1986). Structural realist research represents basic science and usually, as in the case of Lorrain and White (1971), involves a mathematical analysis.

4.1.2 Instrumentalism

A very different approach to research is identified in the bottom right corner of Figure 3 in the form of instrumentalism, also known as problem-solving and pragmatism. For many people, the goal of science is to solve problems (Laudan, 1977). Questions of the truth or falsity of theories are irrelevant. Scientific theories are useful instruments in helping predict events and solve problems (Cartwright, 1983; Friedman, 1953). As Rob Cross and colleagues explained, "[s]ocial network analysis can be an invaluable tool for systematically assessing and then intervening at critical points within an informal network" (Cross, Borgatti, & Parker, 2002: 26). For example, the problem might be how to get ahead in the modern corporation. One answer would be to span across the gaps in the social structure to gain nonredundant knowledge (Burt, 1992). Or, if you are manager of a subunit, you might be faced with the problem of how to gain access to sticky knowledge circulating within other subunits. The answer would be that weak ties are perfectly adequate for the transfer of standardized formulaic information, but strong ties are needed for the transfer of complex knowledge (Hansen, 1999). These influential research endeavors provide specific and valuable answers to important questions.

4.1.3 Foundationalism

A third approach to the science of social networks is provided by foundationalism, captured in the bottom left-hand corner of Figure 3. Foundationalism emphasizes induction, that is, the surfacing of processes and structures that are otherwise invisible. Patterns emerge from the analysis of data according to this scientific approach. The possibility of gathering huge data sets and studying them with high-powered computers gives new impetus to this approach and has fueled the speculation of a post-theory scientific revolution (Spinney, 2022). Social network researchers (e.g., Dorogovtsev & Mendes, 2003) apply their tools to huge data sets that represent interactions on the World Wide Web and neurological networks. These analyses of millions of connections are typically billed as exploratory, meaning that theory emerges from the data (e.g., Ogle, Tenkasi, & Brock, 2020).

4.1.4 Paradigm Extending

The fourth approach, paradigm extending, in the top right-hand corner of Figure 3, differs in that theory drives the search for issues to study. This approach derives from the influential work of Thomas Kuhn concerning the extent to which mature sciences exhibit a distinctive set of taken-for-granted ideas, a community of interacting researchers, specialist conferences, and dedicated journals. Social network research has achieved paradigmatic status according to some leading figures (Hummon & Carley, 1993). If your research endeavor involves working within the assumptions of a leading theory such as structural-hole theory, then your work is paradigmatic. For example, perhaps the puzzle you address is whether social network brokers benefit from second-order social capital, that is, from spanning structural holes between contacts of your primary contacts. This effort helps refine and extend structural-hole theory. Indeed, relevant research on this puzzle shows that returns to brokerage are predominantly derived from spanning primary structural holes, that is, those that separate the people you are directly connected to (Burt, 2007). But second-order social capital does matter when these second-order contacts are with senior brokers (Galunic, Ertug, & Gargiulo, 2012).

Being clear concerning the purpose of your research facilitates the choice of theory, data, and methods. If your goal is to uncover the basic fabric of social network reality, then your choice of methods probably involves advanced mathematics. If your goal is to find patterns in mountains of data, then your goal is best served by atheoretical data mining associated with foundationalism. The pragmatic goal of solving an outstanding problem for an organization allows you to call upon any theory and any method that promises better predictability. But if you seek to contribute within the paradigm of existing theory, then the ideas and methods associated with that theory are to be preferred. In the next set of sections, we provide a guide to some of the basic tools and empirical approaches used by social network researchers.

4.2 Research Design

4.2.1 Whole-Network Design

There are two different approaches to the collection of social network data. As our previous summary of philosophical approaches to research reiterates, the type of social network data you collect depends on the kind of research question you want to answer. The *whole-network* (or *sociocentric*) approach requires collecting *all ties* among those included in the network (Borgatti, Everett, & Johnson, 2018). Under this design, actors in the network provide information concerning their social network connections with all other actors. For example, an analysis of the extent to which brokers who spanned between cliques were trusted involved the collection of two sets of data, one comprising students, and the other comprising hospital workers, as described by the authors (Tasselli & Kilduff, 2018: 808–809):

> *Master's sample*. We surveyed 148 members of a full-time, two-year European business school master's degree program . . .. We presented people with a paper-based questionnaire during the third semester and 126 people (i.e., 85 percent) responded (average work experience = 2.31 years) . . ..
>
> *Hospital*. We surveyed 84 professionals employed in a critical-care unit of a publicly funded European hospital. Work involved diagnosis, surgical intervention, pharmaceutical care, and continuous checks of patients' health conditions. Seventy-five people (20 doctors, 39 nurses, 16 para-medical staff) responded to a paper-based questionnaire (response rate = 89 percent) . . . .
>
> Across both samples, we used the roster method to collect network data (Wasserman & Faust, 1994: 46), an approach that reduces the likelihood that respondents forget important contacts (Marsden, 2011: 372). Each respondent was presented with a complete alphabetical list of all those in the relevant Master's or hospital network and asked to indicate the names of "people you consider as 'friends' – that is people with whom you frequently and regularly have friendly and pleasant relationships during classes and during your stay at the business school" (Master's sample) or "during your stay at work" (Hospital sample).

Whole-network data can also be derived from archival sources as illustrated in this influential examination of embeddedness among 479 firms (Uzzi, 1997: 685):

> Data on the network ties among all better dress apparel firms in the New York apparel economy were obtained from the International Ladies Garment Workers Union, which keeps records on the volume of exchanges between contractors and manufacturers . . .. The data describe (1) firm-to firm resource exchanges, (2) business group membership, and (3) a company's product lines, age, size of employment, and location. The data on resource exchange and social tie networks cover the full network of relations for each firm in this economy (e.g., the proportion of work that each firm "sends" and "receives"

to and from its network partners and whether firms are linked by family, friendship, or shareholdings).

The whole-network design is useful not only for the examination of embeddedness but also for the analysis of structural features of networks that include network *centralization*, that is, the extent to which interactions are concentrated among a small number of actors (Freeman, 1979), and network *density*, that is, the extent to which actors in the network are connected to each other (Wasserman & Faust, 1994). The whole-network design also provides information on the relative centrality or peripherality of each node. For example, the extent to which each node spans across structural holes is captured by *betweenness centrality*, defined as the extent to which each person is on the shortest paths between other actors in the network (Freeman, 1979). Whereas some research reports that central actors are more creative (e.g., Mehra et al., 2001), other research suggests that creativity derives from occupying a position between the core group of centralized actors and the set of peripheral actors that are loosely connected to the core. To test this latter hypothesis, the authors collected whole data on the Hollywood film industry as follows (Cattani & Ferriani, 2008: 829):

> Our data consist of the entire population of core crew members who worked in at least one of the 2,137 movies distributed in the United States by the eight major studios—i.e., the seven historical majors (Universal, Paramount, Warner Bros, Columbia-Tristar, Disney, 20th Century Fox, and Metro-Goldwyn-Mayer) and Dreamworks—and their corresponding subsidiaries over the 12-year period 1992–2003.

Thus, whole-network research both captures the global patterns of connection among all actors, providing insights that are otherwise buried under the plethora of social relations, and allows for the analysis of micro-level phenomena such as the relative centrality of each member of the network.

Unless the whole-network data can be assembled unobtrusively from archival or other sources (e.g., Uzzi, 1997), this design requires that network members be identified, usually by name, so that respondents can report the presence or absence of ties to and from each other. Data can be collected confidentially, but not anonymously. Researchers may have to make extra efforts to increase trust, provide assurances concerning confidentiality, and thereby increase participation. This will help avoid distorted results concerning network structure that can be caused by missing data (Borgatti, Carley, & Krackhardt, 2006).

4.2.2 Ego-Network Design

Different from the whole-network approach, *ego-network* (or *egocentric*) design involves identifying each individual ego's direct contacts and the connections among those contacts (Wasserman & Faust, 1994). People directly connected to ego are called *alters*. Under this design, information concerning alters' characteristics, ego–alter relations, and alter–alter relations can be supplied by ego (e.g., Burt, 2004) or collected unobtrusively from employment records, for example (Burt & Ronchi, 1990). This data collection approach helps answer questions concerning the network ties or networking behavior of egos in a social context.

Ego-network research, indeed, focuses on the local social networks surrounding egos, rather than the full set of relations among all egos and alters. Thus, ego-network research primarily focuses on outcomes related to ego rather than structural features of whole networks. For example, controlling for the size of ego's network and for the extent to which ego's network features a rival who connects to many of ego's contacts, we can calculate the extent to which ego's alters are directly connected to each other with *network constraint*, a measure of social network brokerage that predicts speed of promotions and other advantageous outcomes (Burt, 1992). Figures 4a and 4b illustrate the ego networks for Avery and Carol. In these two ego networks, we see that Avery is a friend of Chris, Carol, and Emily, who are also friends of each other. By contrast, in Carol's network, some people, such as Jack and Emily, are not friends. Thus, Carol has a brokerage role whereas Avery does not.

Ego-network research typically offers little insight regarding global patterns of connections (Perry, Pescosolido, & Borgatti, 2018) unless the researcher aggregates the different ego networks into a whole network (e.g., Burt, 2004). Ego-network research is particularly useful for accessing network data on individuals located in relatively large organizations. A whole-network approach would burden each respondent with the necessity of recalling connections among hundreds or even thousands of alters. To achieve a balance between the completeness and the quality of data, researchers often limit the number of

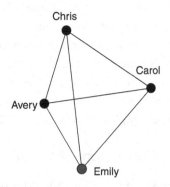

Figure 4a Avery's ego network.

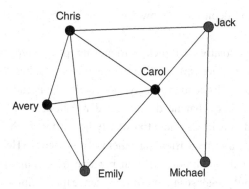

Figure 4b Carol's ego network.

alters to be listed by egos (e.g., Brands & Mehra, 2019). Missing data in an ego-network design is less problematic than in a whole-network design.

As mentioned already, ego networks can be combined to construct a whole network (Weeks et al., 2002). Even if ego-network data are collected anonymously, alters listed by different egos may be identified and matched based on the alters' attributes, such as demographic information, with the aid of software packages like SPIDER (Semi-automated Processing of Interconnected Dyads using Entity Resolution; Young & Hopkins, 2015). But researchers should be cautious about possible errors in the process of identifying alters (Perry et al., 2018). And there are ethical and legal constraints on the identification of individuals with which researchers must comply.

4.2.3 Cognitive Social Structure Design

Cognitive social structure (CSS) research represents a different perspective to data collection from the two previous approaches in that individuals provide *perceptions* of network ties between every possible pair in the network (e.g., Kilduff & Krackhardt, 1994). This allows researchers to compare each individual's perception of the network with the actual network of ties. Actual ties can be defined as those that are verified by both people involved in the tie (e.g., Krackhardt, 1987). That is, if John reports in his cognitive map that Avery claims friendship with Jane, then both Avery and Jane must agree that there is a one-way tie from Avery to Jane for this tie to be considered an actual tie rather than John's perception of a tie. In cases of very large networks where this CSS procedure proves too onerous, perceptions can be gathered from each person concerning a subset of their fellow network members' network connections (e.g, Flynn et al., 2006). Or respondents can select from a set of stylized network structures a visual depiction of how they perceive the network (Mehra et al., 2014).

In reporting on positive ties such as friendship, people typically inflate their own centrality in the network relative to how others see them (e.g., Kumbasar et al., 1994). People also tend to perceive both their own friendship relations and those of distant others as balanced (Krackhardt & Kilduff, 1999), that is, as both reciprocated and transitive, where transitivity here refers to the perception that people who have a mutual friend are themselves friends (Heider, 1958). We should note that the common research practice of symmetrizing friendship relations to simplify analyses ignores the evidence that reciprocity in friendship relationships is likely to be less than 50 percent in organizational settings (Krackhardt & Kilduff, 1999).

CSS research focuses not just on misperceptions concerning reciprocity and other structural features of networks (Brands, 2013; Krackhardt, 1987) but also on the outcomes related to these misperceptions. For example, an analysis of the effects of having actual versus perceived prominent friends showed that being perceived by others to have a prominent friend in an organization increased an individual's performance reputation, whereas having such a friend had no effect (Kilduff & Krackhardt, 1994).

4.3 Sampling and Bounding Networks

The identification of social network boundaries is a critical step in network research (see Agneessens & Labianca, 2022 for a discussion). Sometimes, a group has an easily observed boundary, such as an organizational department (e.g., Kumbasar et al., 1994). In other cases, boundary specification requires compiling a list of the members of the population, collecting all the direct and possibly indirect ties of interest to the researcher (e.g., Powell et al., 1996), and establishing the period over which the data will be collected. For example, a study of the spread of poison pills through the US intercorporate network used the Fortune 500 list of companies as the initial boundary set but had to exclude forty-two companies that featured missing data and thirty-two firms that were not publicly traded (Davis, 1991). The time interval was fixed as between 1984 and 1989. The network measure of interest was a board interlock. These data on ties between companies had to be checked against standard directories even though initial data collection used computerized routines.

Similarly, with an ego-network design, participants and their alters need to be identified. One source of ego-network data is the US 1985 General Social Survey (GSS), a national probability sample of 1,395 adults. To investigate the extent to which, under job threat, status affects network recall, researchers reduced this sample to 806 people through the elimination of data from the nonemployed and the exclusion from the sample of respondents for whom other necessary data were missing (Smith, Menon, & Thompson, 2012). The GSS ego-network data were collected using the following name-generator question and follow-up probing:

> "From time to time, most people discuss important matters with other people. Looking back over the last six months—who are the people with whom you discussed matters important to you?" Interviewers probed for additional names when respondents named fewer than five people. Additionally, respondents described the presence or lack of relationship between each of the contacts named (Smith et al., 2012: 72).

In other cases, snowball sampling can help establish the boundary of the network beyond the initial sample of people identified by the researcher. The process involves collecting information on the contacts of the original sample members and continuing to collect information on the contacts of the contacts until few new names are added to the sample (Scott, 2000: 61). This process provides reasonable estimates of dyads and triads in the larger population of interest (Frank, 1978, 1979).

4.4 Data Collection

4.4.1 Data Sources

If we are interested in understanding the communication networks within an organization, a straightforward way is to survey employees and ask them to report their networks (e.g., Burt & Wang, 2021; Tasselli & Kilduff, 2018; Soda, Tortoriello, & Iorio, 2018; Landis et al., 2018). We can also collect network data from archival sources (Burt & Lin, 1977). For example, email exchange records can capture interpersonal social networks in organizations (e.g., Quintane & Carnabuci, 2016; Kleinbaum, Stuart, & Tushman, 2013). Other archival data is either stored in organizations' databases or available online. For example, to construct the coach social networks in the National Football League (NFL) over thirty years, Kilduff et al. (2016) used the Record and Fact Book and cross-referenced other online archival data such as Pro Football Reference (www.pro-football-reference.com). The collection of secondary data and the hand coding of these data are often time-consuming activities but allow the researcher to avoid problems related to obtrusive research methods (Webb et al., 1999).

Social network research can also involve the observation of interactions between people (e.g., Whyte, 1943), the interviewing of people about their network relationships (e.g., Burt, 1984), and the analysis of how people randomly assigned to different network setups interact with each other (e.g., Freeman, Roeder, & Mulholland, 1979). Contemporary network research often features a combination of types of study including surveys and experiments, thereby helping establish the validity and reliability of the research (e.g., Casciaro, Gino, & Kouchaki, 2014; Landis et al., 2018).

4.4.2 Data Collection Techniques

What methods are used in the collection of social network data? The answer depends, to some extent, on the research design. The *roster method* (Wasserman & Faust, 1994) is widely used in whole-network research (e.g., Tasselli, 2015; Tasselli, Zappa, & Lomi, 2020; Kleinbaum, Jordan, & Audia, 2015; Tortoriello, Reagans, & McEvily, 2012). This method involves presenting research respondents with a complete list of people who are included in the predetermined network boundary such as an organizational department. Then respondents indicate their social connections with the people on the roster. For example, we could ask respondents to indicate those people on the roster whom they consider to be their friends (e.g., Tasselli & Kilduff, 2018). This approach helps respondents recall their interactions with all relevant important contacts (Marsden, 2011), thereby avoiding well-known problems with respondent recall (Freeman et al., 1987).

The other approach, *name generator* (or *free recall*, Wasserman & Faust, 1994), is normally used in research with an ego-network design (e.g., Soda et al., 2018; Cross & Cummings, 2004; Battilana & Casciaro, 2012). Using this method, researchers construct egocentric social network data by asking respondents to freely recall and write down the names of people (i.e., alters) in the network. A name generator is used together with *name interpreters* to elicit the attributes of each listed alter, the network features (such as tie strength) between egos and alters, and the network features among alters (Perry et al., 2018).

An example of this egocentric technique is taken from an article on second-hand brokerage that involved the following procedure concerning the relationships among supply-chain managers (Burt, 2007: 127). Managers were asked to describe their best idea for improving supply-chain operations and then asked if they had discussed the idea with anyone. If yes, they were asked to name the person. Next, they were asked, "More generally, who are the people with whom you most often discuss supply-chain issues?" The respondent was then guided through a matrix in which the respondent's perceived relation between each pair of contacts was coded as "often," "sometimes," or "rarely" in regard to how often the two contacts discussed supply-chain issues.

As well as being used in studies with an ego-network design, a name generator can also be used as a complement to the roster approach to identify relevant social contacts omitted from the roster due to the limitation of the prespecified research boundary (e.g., Rodan & Galunic, 2004).

4.5 Visualization Using Graphs

Imagine that your research project requires you to represent the friendship network among employees within a research and development (R&D) department and to understand the connections between this network and the innovation activities of the firm. You have already thought through the theoretical approach that will best help you approach your research question. Now, it is time to think about methods and visualization. How do you go about doing this? One intuitive way to represent any set of relationships among people is to draw a graph. Graphs have long been used for the visualization of social network relationships (e.g., Roethlisberger & Dickson, 1939), but they also capture the data necessary for systematic analysis. The theory of graphs provides systematic vocabulary and mathematical operations to describe, denote, and quantify network structural features (Harary, Norman, & Cartwright, 1965). In this section, we illustrate basic graph theoretical concepts.

In a graph, *nodes* (or *points* or *vertices*) represent actors in a social network, for example Avery and Chris in Figure 5a. *Ties* (or *lines* or *edges*) between two nodes represent social relations, for example friendship, in this case. Two nodes are *adjacent* if they are directly linked by a tie, and the number of adjacent nodes is called the *degree* of a node. For example, in Figure 5a Jack is adjacent to Chris, Carol, and Michael. Jack has three connections, hence a network degree of three.

Ties within a specific graph represent a single type of relationship. For example, a friendship network is represented in Figure 5a, whereas Figure 5b represents a task communication network. Some types of social relation, such as

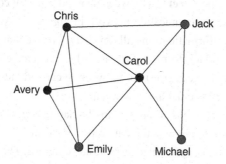

Figure 5a Friendship network.

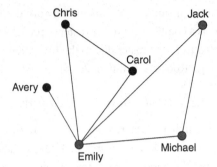

Figure 5b Task communication network.

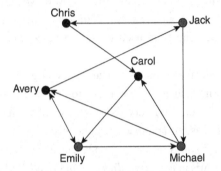

Figure 5c Advice-giving network.

talks with, tend to be reciprocated, whereas other types of social relation, such as *gives advice*, are directed from one person to another person without reciprocation. An example of a directed tie is represented in Figure 5c in which the one-way arrow from Avery to Jack shows the flow of advice. If two persons, such as Avery and Emily, advise each other, the tie is represented by a double-headed arrow.

Some actors have no direct ties between them but can still connect via others. For example, in the communication network in Figure 5b, Avery and Jack are not connected, but information can still flow between Avery and Jack via Emily. Thus, Avery–Emily–Jack forms a *path*, namely, a sequence of nodes without revisiting. This path is the shortest one between Avery and Jack and is defined as the *geodesic distance* (or *distance*) between them.

The information in graphs is captured mathematically in *adjacency matrices*. For example, Figure 6 contains the data represented in Figure 5c. In an adjacency matrix, nodes are represented by rows and columns. The tie from node *i* to node *j* is indicated by the entry in row *i* and column *j*. For example, Avery's

	Avery	Chris	Emily	Jack	Michael	Carol
Avery	0	0	1	1	0	0
Chris	0	0	0	0	0	1
Emily	1	0	0	0	1	0
Jack	0	1	0	0	1	0
Michael	1	0	0	0	0	1
Carol	0	0	1	0	0	0

Figure 6 Matrix of binary advice-giving relationships.

	Avery	Chris	Emily	Jack	Michael	Carol
Avery	0	0	1	1	0	0
Chris	0	0	0	0	0	1
Emily	1	0	0	0	3	0
Jack	0	2	0	0	1	0
Michael	1	0	0	0	0	1
Carol	0	0	2	0	0	0

Figure 7 Matrix of valued advice-giving relationships.

advice-giving to Jack is indicated by "1" in Row 1, Column 4 in Figure 6. The matrix diagonal is filled with zeros by convention unless people's ties to themselves are well-defined.

The graphs and matrices capture the presence or absence of relationships between people either in binary terms – zeros and ones – or in more nuanced terms to indicate the relative strength of relationships. For example, in the matrix depicted in Figure 7, a higher number indicates a stronger tie in terms of higher frequency of advice-giving. In a graph, there are also multiple ways of visualizing the features of social connections, such as adding value on top of lines, or adjusting tie width according to tie strength, as shown in Figure 8.

4.6 Data Analysis

4.6.1 Characterizing Networks: Centrality

Social network analyses allow us to understand the structural characteristics of whole networks and the structural features of each individual's network position. In this section, we focus on one of the most important node-level properties in social network analyses: *centrality*. Centrality incorporates a set of concepts that indicate different aspects of individuals' structural importance in social networks (Borgatti 2005; Borgatti & Everett, 2006). In undirected networks, the widely used centrality measures include degree centrality,

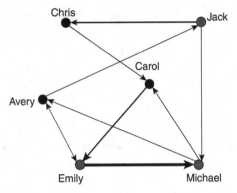

Figure 8 Advice-giving network with values indicated by line thickness.

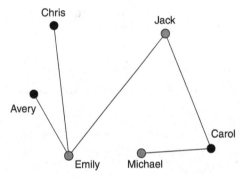

Figure 9 Idea-sharing network.

eigenvector centrality, betweenness centrality, and closeness centrality. We introduce each of these four measures next and summarize their equations and interpretations in Table 2.

Degree centrality (Freeman, 1979; Wang et al., 2014; O'Mahony & Ferraro, 2007) can be thought of as an actor's popularity in that it comprises a count of each actor's ties. For example, in the idea-sharing network illustrated in Figure 9, Emily shares ideas with three persons, that is, Avery, Chris, and Jack. Thus, Emily's degree centrality in this network equals three. Degree centrality indicates the extent to which an actor is visible in the network and the extent to which an actor is exposed to emotional support, work-related advice, gossip, disease, good ideas, and other influences (Borgatti et al., 2018).

Betweenness centrality (Freeman, 1977; e.g., Tasselli & Kilduff, 2018) captures how often a given actor occupies a network position that falls on the shortest path between two other actors. This measure of centrality is interpreted as an actor's potential to play the role of a gatekeeper who can control flows

Table 2 Summary of centrality measures.

Measure	Equation	Interpretation
Degree centrality	$d_i = \sum_j x_{ij}$, where d_i is the degree centrality of actor i, and x_{ij} is the value in row i and column j of the adjacency matrix.	Popularity and exposure to flows through the network; direct opportunity to influence or be influenced
Betweenness centrality	$b_i = \sum_{h<j} \frac{g_{hij}}{g_{hj}}$, where b_i is the betweenness centrality of actor i, g_{hij} is the number of geodesic paths that link h and j via i, and g_{hj} is the total number of geodesic paths that link h and j.	Control over things flowing through the network (gatekeeping; brokering)
Closeness centrality (normalized)	$c_i = (n-1)/[\sum_j d(i,j)]$, where c_i is the closeness centrality of actor i, n is the number of nodes in the network, and $d(i,j)$ is the geodesic distance from i to j.	The speed at which an actor receives things flowing through the network

Table 2 (cont.)

Measure	Equation	Interpretation
Eigenvector centrality	Let X be the adjacency matrix of a network, λ the largest eigenvalue of X, and $\mathbf{e}$ the eigenvector: $X\mathbf{e} = \lambda\mathbf{e}$, thus, $\mathbf{e} = \frac{1}{\lambda}X\mathbf{e}$. Then the i_{th} component of $\mathbf{e}$ gives the eigenvector centrality of actor i: $e_i = \frac{1}{\lambda}\sum_j x_{ij}e_j$, where e_i is the eigenvector centrality of actor i, and x_{ij} is the value in row i and column j of the adjacency matrix.	The well-connectedness of each actor, often interpreted as status

through networks (Brass, 1984). For example, actors with high betweenness centrality can filter or distort information flowing via them, and can separate or liaise between disconnected alters (Borgatti, Everett, & Johnson, 2013). As such, betweenness centrality can be used as a measure of brokerage if the size of each individual's network is controlled for (e.g., Oh & Kilduff, 2008). For egocentric research, the appropriate measure is *ego betweenness*, which is specific to the set of actors directly connected to ego. Based on the equation in Table 2, Emily's betweenness centrality in the team's idea-sharing network is seven, whereas Carol's is four. Thus, compared with Carol, Emily has more control over the ideas flowing within this team.

Closeness centrality (Freeman, 1979; e.g., Perry-Smith, 2006; Tsai, 2001) is often normalized in use and captures the distance between one actor and other actors in a network. It equals the reverse of the sum of geodesic distances between an actor and others. This value is then multiplied by $n-1$ for normalization, with n representing the number of nodes in a network. A higher closeness centrality indicates that an actor can reach other actors quickly via a smaller number of links (Borgatti, 2005). Based on the equation in Table 2, Chris's closeness centrality in the team's idea-sharing network is 0.42, whereas Jack's is 0.63. Thus, Jack is likely to hear new ideas shared in this network more quickly than Chris. Note that in networks that include two completely disconnected actors, the distance between them is not well-defined and closeness centrality cannot be calculated directly. A few options are available to address this issue, such as recoding the distance as the number of nodes (Freeman, 1979) or setting the reverse distance as zero (Valente & Foreman, 1998).

Eigenvector centrality captures the idea that some network contacts are more important than others. It is similar to degree centrality in terms of indicating actors' exposure to flows through the network, but it has been described as a type of "turbo-charged" degree centrality (Borgatti et al., 2013). Unlike degree centrality, which considers each actor to be connected equally with the focal actor, the eigenvector measure assigns a weight to each actor being directly linked to the focal actor (Bonacich, 1972; e.g., Jensen & Wang, 2018; Shipilov, Greve, & Rowley, 2010). Specifically, a person's eigenvector centrality is a weighted sum of eigenvector centralities of this person's adjacent contacts. The intuition behind this measure is that the centrality of an actor, for example Avery, depends not only on how many actors Avery is connected to but also on whether Avery knows influential others who are also central in the network (Bonacich, 2007).

Eigenvector centrality is often interpreted as a person's status in a network. For example, in the idea-sharing network in Figure 9, Avery is connected to Emily, and Michael is connected to Carol. Thus, Avery's and Michael's degree centralities are both equal to one. But Avery's single contact, Emily, is a prominent member of the network in that she has three connections. Thus, Avery has higher eigenvector centrality than Michael because of her link to the well-connected Emily.

Measuring centrality is more complicated in directed networks where relationships between two actors may be asymmetric. Whereas betweenness centrality can be used in directed networks, the other three measures require adjustments. The basic principle of these adjustments is to consider the network as having two versions, with each version representing one direction of the network. For example, for degree centrality, in the directed advice-giving network shown in Figure 5c, we could calculate Carol's *indegree* centrality, which reflects how much advice she receives from others, and *outdegree* centrality, which reflects how much advice she gives to others (Wasserman & Faust, 1994). A similar approach applies to eigenvalue centrality and closeness centrality (Borgatti et al., 2018).

4.6.2 Network Structures

Network research is often referred to as structural analysis (e.g., Kilduff & Krackhardt, 1994) in deference to its emphasis on discerning and analyzing structural features of the social world. In this section, we discuss some of the basic structures that feature in social networks.

A *dyad* consists of two actors between whom there is either a tie or an absence of a tie (Wasserman & Faust, 1994). Figure 10 shows the three possible dyadic states: *null*, that is, no tie; *asymmetric*, that is, a one-way tie; and *reciprocated*, that is, a two-way tie. An asymmetric positive one-way relationship such as friendship or resource provision may provoke an impetus for the relationship to be reciprocated or disbanded to restore balance (Heider, 1958; Wellman, 1988). Across a social network, the extent of reciprocity can be measured as the proportion of reciprocated ties relative to all ties. For example, in the advice network displayed in Figure 5c, only the tie between Avery and Emily is

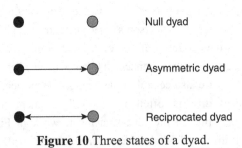

Figure 10 Three states of a dyad.

reciprocated, meaning that overall reciprocity is 11 percent. Low reciprocity in a network may indicate status hierarchy, with some high-status actors receiving many nominations that they do not reciprocate.

Triads. Long considered the building blocks of informal networks (Holland & Leinhardt, 1977), triads involve three actors and the presence or absence of ties among them. Triads, relative to dyads, provide for the possibility of alliances (two against one), brokerage (one brokering between the other two), and the formation of majorities and minorities (Simmel, 1950).

Balance theory (Heider, 1958) alerts us to the importance of triadic *transitivity* in positive relationships such as friendship. Ignoring cases of vacuous transitivity involving, for example, three isolates, transitivity refers to whether the triad is complete. For example, if Ann regards both Bill and Colin as her friends, then the triad is transitive if Bill and Colin are friends with each other. The transitivity principle is important in weak-tie theory, where a friendship group of three people in which the link between two is missing is labeled the *forbidden triad*, forbidden because of the assumption of strong pressure on two people who have a mutual friend to become friends (Granovetter, 1973).

The members of a dyad embedded within a triad (i.e., Simmelian dyads – Krackhardt, 1998, 1999) are constrained in their attitudes and behaviors because of their connections to a third party according to theory (Simmel, 1950) and empirical research (Krackhardt, 1998; Krackhardt & Kilduff, 2002). But if a person is embedded in more than one such triad, the person may gain new ideas and access to resources by virtue of being a "multiple insider" – someone who benefits from the cohesion available within closed groups and the nonredundancy that comes from being able to move across such groups (Vedres & Stark, 2010).

A *clique* refers to a complete network in which every actor is directly connected to every other actor and has no common link to anyone outside the clique (Luce & Perry, 1949). For example, Figure 11 illustrates the interaction network among fourteen participants and four instructors at a National Science Foundation summer camp in 1992 (Borgatti, Everett, & Freeman, 1999). There are ten cliques in the camp. Cliques may emerge based on shared demographic characteristics such as gender and ethnicity (e.g., Mehra et al., 1998). People who bridge two or more cliques are *Simmelian brokers* (Krackhardt, 1999) who may face paralyzing pressures to conform (Krackhardt, 1999: 206) or who may find themselves liberated to pursue innovative activities (Vedres & Stark, 2010) based on how well their dispositions are matched to the brokerage challenge of moving between different closed groups (Tasselli & Kilduff, 2018).

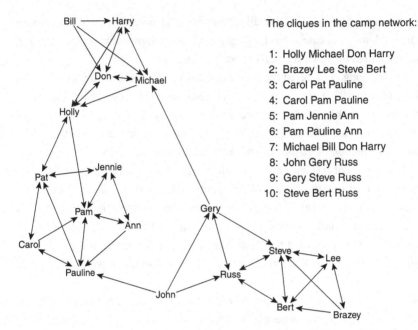

The cliques in the camp network:

1: Holly Michael Don Harry
2: Brazey Lee Steve Bert
3: Carol Pat Pauline
4: Carol Pam Pauline
5: Pam Jennie Ann
6: Pam Pauline Ann
7: Michael Bill Don Harry
8: John Gery Russ
9: Gery Steve Russ
10: Steve Bert Russ

Figure 11 Interaction networks and cliques in the National Science Foundation summer camp.

Centralization refers to the extent to which a network is centralized around one or a few actors. It is measured as a ratio of actors' centrality scores, most typically their degree centrality scores (Freeman, 1979). The nominator is the sum of the difference between the most central node's centrality and every other node's centrality, whereas the denominator is the maximum possible centralization score for that network. The maximum centralization occurs in a star network (one actor connected to all others with no other connections between actors) as illustrated in Figure 12. In the help network shown in Figure 13, the most central person is Carol, whose degree centrality is five. Thus, the nominator = 16: (5−1) + (5−2) + (5−2) + (5−2) + (5−2) + (5−5), whereas the denominator = 20: (5−1) + (5−1) + (5−1) + (5−1) + (5−1) + (5−5), and the centralization score = 16/20 = 0.8. By contrast, the camp social network in Figure 11 has no centralized actors so the centralization score is 7 percent.

As an important network structural feature, network centralization affects both individual and organizational outcomes. For example, in a longitudinal study that examined how social networks influenced the effectiveness of enterprise system implementation, researchers found that centralized structures made the implementation more likely to fail (Sasidharan et al., 2012). But at the individual level, employees with high indegree centrality reported

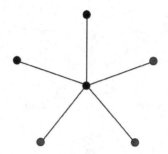

Figure 12 A star network with six nodes.

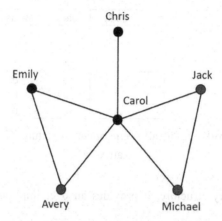

Figure 13 A help network with six nodes.

implementation success even when they worked in centralized units. Thus, individual centrality and network centralization jointly affected people's self-perceptions of success.

Networks can be assessed as to the extent to which they exhibit a *core/periphery* structure, which, in the extreme, features core members connected to everyone and periphery members connected only to core members and not to other members of the periphery (Borgatti & Everett, 2000). In Figure 14, Emily, Chris, and Avery are the core actors, whereas the other three are peripheral actors.

There are two ways of identifying core/periphery structures in social networks (Borgatti et al., 2018). The discrete method involves an optimization process: Actors are assigned to be either core or peripheral such that the correlation between the data matrix and the ideal matrix is maximized, indicated by a measure of fit. This optimization makes sure that the partition of core and peripheral actors maximizes the core–core ties and minimizes the periphery–periphery ties. Although this method matches the essential features

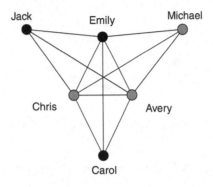

	Avery	Chris	Emily	Jack	Michael	Carol
Avery	1	1	1	1	1	1
Chris	1	1	1	1	1	1
Emily	1	1	1	1	1	1
Jack	1	1	1	0	0	0
Michael	1	1	1	0	0	0
Carol	1	1	1	0	0	0

Figure 14 A network with ideal core/periphery structure: Graph and network matrix.

of a core/periphery structure, it provides an oversimplified description of network structure.

The continuous method provides a more comprehensive picture of the extent of core/periphery structuring. This method generates a node-level coreness value by modelling the existence or strength of ties between a pair of actors i and j as a function of the coreness of each actor. If we use x_{ij} to denote the entry of row i and column j in a network matrix A^*, and use c_i to denote the coreness of actors i, this method sets x_{ij} equal to $c_i c_j$. If both actors have high coreness, they are connected; and if both actors have low coreness, they are not connected. Then a least-squared procedure is implemented to identify coreness scores for each actor to minimize the Euclidean distance between the real data matrix A and the matrix A^*. For example, Figure 15 illustrates the interaction network among workers in negotiation for higher wages in a tailor shop in Zambia (Kapferer 1972) and the list of people with the highest and lowest coreness scores generated based on the continuous method.

In organizations, core/periphery positions expose people to trade-offs between resource support and fresh ideas. Core people in organizations are likely to obtain the resources and legitimacy that are essential to achieving

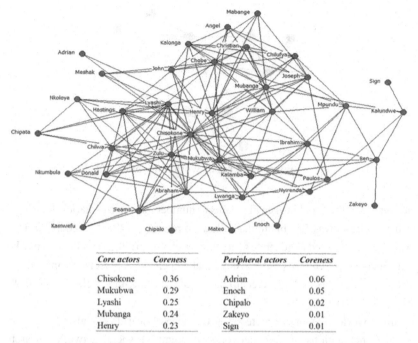

Core actors	Coreness	Peripheral actors	Coreness
Chisokone	0.36	Adrian	0.06
Mukubwa	0.29	Enoch	0.05
Lyashi	0.25	Chipalo	0.02
Mubanga	0.24	Zakeyo	0.01
Henry	0.23	Sign	0.01

Figure 15 Time 1 interaction networks of Zambian workers (Kapferer, 1972).

success (e.g., Hargadon, 2006). But peripheral people are theorized by some researchers as likely to generate new ideas because they face less pressure to conform to field norms (Perry-Smith & Shalley, 2003). The creativity of peripheral actors was summarized by polymath Michael Polanyi (1963: 1013) as follows: "I would never have conceived my theory, let alone have made a great effort to verify it, if I had been more familiar with major developments in physics that were taking place." An alternative view is that higher creative performance is found among people who occupy an intermediate core/periphery position in their organizations (Cattani & Ferriani, 2008).

Small-world networks are characterized by high local clustering and short average paths (Watts & Strogatz, 1998). Local clustering means that actors in the network tend to be well connected within several distinct clusters, and short average path-length means that any actor in the network can reach any other actor via a small number of intermediate actors. Figure 16 illustrates an example of a small-world network. In the classic small-world research conducted by Travers and Milgram (1969), researchers invited 396 people in Nebraska and Boston to mail a folder directly to a Boston-area stockbroker if they personally knew this individual, or to mail the folder to a personal acquaintance who might know the individual. In this study, sixty-four folders were successfully

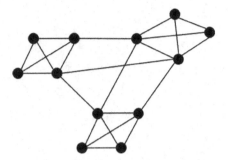

Figure 16 A small-world network.

delivered to the stockbroker. The mean number of intermediaries for these delivery chains was 5.2. In similar follow-up research, 540 white people in Los Angeles were invited to generate acquaintance chains to either a white- or a black-target person in New York. It turned out that 33 percent of persons completed the white-target chains and 13 percent completed the black-target chains (Korte & Milgram 1970).

Small-world networks are features of the real world, but also feature in people's perceptions of their networks. A cognitive social network research effort showed that, given the difficulties in organizing and tracking even small social networks in organizations, people used small world principles in their perceptions of friendship networks. People perceived their work colleagues as interacting in dense clusters, with connections across the clusters between the most popular people within the clusters. The actual networks showed no features of small-worldness whereas the perceived networks exhibited small-world features of clustering and connectivity (Kilduff et al., 2008).

To understand the extent to which a network displays small-world properties, we calculate the *small-world quotient* (Watts & Strogatz, 1998) as illustrated in Table 3. The quotient is made up of two criteria: the extent to which the network shows much higher clustering than a random network of the same size, and the average path-length. The *clustering coefficient* measures the average interconnectedness of ego's alters in a network. Take a friendship network, for example: the clustering coefficient equals the extent to which ego's friends are also friends of each other, averaged across all egos in the network (Watts, 1999). The path-length between two actors in a network equals the smallest number of ties that an actor needs to traverse to reach the other actor (Watts & Strogatz, 1998). Taking the average of all individual path-lengths between all connected individual actors generates the average *path-length* in a network. The clustering coefficient and average path-length values are then adjusted to account for the properties of a random network of the same size and density, because dense networks exhibit

Table 3 Formula for small-world quotient.

Variable	Formula
Clustering coefficient (CC)	$\sum_{i=1}^{n} \frac{C_i}{n}$, where $C_i = \frac{A_i}{k_i(k_i-1)}$ and A_i is the actual number of ties between node i's k_i adjacent nodes
Expected network clustering coefficient (CC_expected)	k/n, where n is the number of nodes in a network and k is the average number of ties per node
Clustering coefficient ratio (CC_ratio)	$CC/CC_{expected}$
Path-length (PL)	$\frac{2}{n(n-1)} \sum_{i=1}^{n} \sum_{j=1}^{n} L_{min}(i,j)$, where L_{min} is the minimum path-length connecting node i and node j
Expected network path-length (PL_expected)	$\ln(n)/\ln(k)$, where n is the number of nodes in a network and k is the average number of ties per node
Path-length ratio (PL_ratio)	$PL/PL_{expected}$
Small-world quotient (*SW*)	CC_{ratio}/PL_{ratio}

more clustering and shorter path-lengths. In a random network with n nodes and k average ties per node, the *expected clustering coefficient* is k/n, and the *expected path-length* is $\ln(n)/\ln(k)$ (Dorogovtsev & Mendes, 2003). The *actual clustering coefficient* and the *actual path-length* are divided by the corresponding expected values, generating a *clustering coefficient ratio* and a *path-length ratio*. The ratio of these two ratios then produces the small-world quotient (e.g., Kilduff et al., 2008).

4.6.3 Duality of Network Structure: Two-Mode Networks

A two-mode network captures the intersection of persons within groups and of groups within individuals (Breiger, 1974). For example, the Southern Women data set (Davis, Gardner, & Gardner, 1941) features eighteen women's attendance at fourteen events, with data collected from newspaper records. Figure 17 shows the network matrix, with the rows representing the women and the columns representing the events. An entry of "1" means that the person attended the event, and "0" means nonattendance.

Two-mode network data can be converted to one-mode data to infer relationships among a single set of entities (Borgatti et al., 2018). In the women–event data set example, we can construct a women–women network based on how many events two women both attended. Figure 18 shows the valued data matrix (with the first two letters representing the corresponding person in the column headings) and the graph (with the co-membership values reflected by the thickness of the lines). We can also construct an event–event network based on how many members are shared by two events, as shown in Figure 19.

Two-mode affiliation data are used in organizational research on topics such as interlocking directorates (e.g., Davis & Greve, 1997) and project collaborations

	E1	E2	E3	E4	E5	E6	E7	E8	E9	E10	E11	E12	E13	E14
Evelyn	1	1	1	1	1	1	0	1	1	0	0	0	0	0
Laura	1	1	1	0	1	1	1	1	0	0	0	0	0	0
Theresa	0	1	1	1	1	1	1	1	1	0	0	0	0	0
Brenda	1	0	1	1	1	1	1	1	0	0	0	0	0	0
Charlotte	0	0	1	1	1	0	1	0	0	0	0	0	0	0
Frances	0	0	1	0	1	1	0	1	0	0	0	0	0	0
Eleanor	0	0	0	0	1	1	1	1	0	0	0	0	0	0
Pearl	0	0	0	0	0	1	0	1	1	0	0	0	0	0
Ruth	0	0	0	0	1	0	1	1	1	0	0	0	0	0
Verne	0	0	0	0	0	0	1	1	1	0	0	1	0	0
Myrna	0	0	0	0	0	0	0	1	1	1	0	1	0	0
Katherine	0	0	0	0	0	0	0	1	1	1	0	1	1	1
Sylvia	0	0	0	0	0	0	1	1	1	1	0	1	1	1
Nora	0	0	0	0	0	1	1	0	1	1	1	1	1	1
Helen	0	0	0	0	0	0	1	1	0	1	1	1	0	0
Dorothy	0	0	0	0	0	0	0	1	1	0	0	0	0	0
Olivia	0	0	0	0	0	0	0	0	1	0	1	0	0	0
Flora	0	0	0	0	0	0	0	0	1	0	1	0	0	0

Figure 17 Two-mode women–event dataset.

	Ev	La	Th	Br	Ch	Fr	El	Pe	Ru	Ve	My	Ka	Sy	No	He	Do	Ol	Fl
Evelyn	8	6	7	6	3	4	3	3	3	2	2	2	2	2	1	2	1	1
Laura	6	7	6	6	3	4	4	2	3	2	1	1	2	2	2	1	0	0
Theresa	7	6	8	6	4	4	4	3	4	3	2	2	3	3	2	2	1	1
Brenda	6	6	6	7	4	4	4	2	3	2	1	1	2	2	2	1	0	0
Charlotte	3	3	4	4	4	2	2	0	2	1	0	0	1	1	1	0	0	0
Frances	4	4	4	4	2	4	3	2	2	1	1	1	1	1	1	1	0	0
Eleanor	3	4	4	4	2	3	4	2	3	2	1	1	2	2	2	1	0	0
Pearl	3	2	3	2	0	2	2	3	2	2	2	2	2	2	1	2	1	1
Ruth	3	3	4	3	2	2	3	2	4	3	2	2	3	2	2	1	1	1
Verne	2	2	3	2	1	1	2	2	3	4	3	3	4	3	3	2	1	1
Myrna	2	1	2	1	0	1	1	2	2	3	4	4	4	3	3	2	1	1
Katherine	2	1	2	1	0	1	1	2	2	3	4	6	6	5	3	2	1	1
Sylvia	2	2	3	2	1	1	2	2	3	4	4	6	7	6	4	2	1	1
Nora	2	2	3	2	1	1	2	2	3	3	3	5	6	8	4	1	2	2
Helen	1	2	2	2	1	1	2	1	2	3	3	3	4	4	5	1	1	1
Dorothy	2	1	2	1	0	1	1	2	2	2	2	2	2	1	1	2	1	1
Olivia	1	0	1	0	0	0	0	1	1	1	1	1	1	1	2	1	2	2
Flora	1	0	1	0	0	0	0	1	1	1	1	1	1	2	1	1	2	2

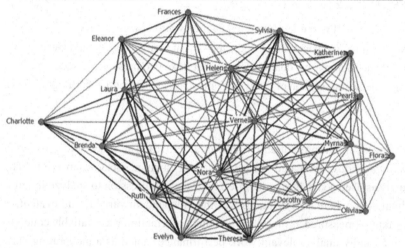

Figure 18 Converted women–women network matrix and graph.

(e.g., Cattani & Ferriani, 2008; Uzzi & Spiro, 2005). Both actors and the places where they interact can be depicted in the same representation using correspondence analysis (e.g., Kilduff & Brass, 2010).

4.6.4 Testing Hypotheses

Standard analytical models are useful if analyses involve network features (e.g., centrality, constraint) at the node level (e.g., person, department, organization) as dependent or independent variables (e.g., Tasselli et al., 2020; Venkataramani et al., 2016; Tortoriello, McEvily, & Krackhardt, 2015). For example, one research effort examined coaches' career trajectories in the NFL over thirty-one years to test whether having a workplace connection to a prestigious industry leader (i.e., an *acolyte* connection) affected a coach's probability of

	E1	E2	E3	E4	E5	E6	E7	E8	E9	E1	E1	E1	E1	E1
E1	3	2	3	2	3	3	2	3	1	0	0	0	0	0
E2	2	3	3	2	3	3	2	3	2	0	0	0	0	0
E3	3	3	6	4	6	5	4	5	2	0	0	0	0	0
E4	2	2	4	4	4	3	3	3	2	0	0	0	0	0
E5	3	3	6	4	8	6	6	7	3	0	0	0	0	0
E6	3	3	5	3	6	8	5	7	4	1	1	1	1	1
E7	2	2	4	3	6	5	10	8	5	3	2	4	2	2
E8	3	3	5	3	7	7	8	14	9	4	1	5	2	2
E9	1	2	2	2	3	4	5	9	12	4	3	5	3	3
E10	0	0	0	0	0	1	3	4	4	5	2	5	3	3
E11	0	0	0	0	0	1	2	1	3	2	4	2	1	1
E12	0	0	0	0	0	1	4	5	5	5	2	6	3	3
E13	0	0	0	0	0	1	2	2	3	3	1	3	3	3
E14	0	0	0	0	0	1	2	2	3	3	1	3	3	3

Figure 19 Converted event–event network matrix.

Note that the women–women and event–event matrices are not independent of each other but involve duality: The tie that links two persons is a set of events forming the intersection of the events' attendance (Simmel, 1955; Breiger, 1974).

getting an initial promotion (Kilduff et al., 2016). The independent variable, *acolyte status*, indicated the existence of such a social connection. The analysis used a standard random-effect logistic regression to analyze longitudinal data, where acolyte status was the independent variable and evaluative certainty (measured as the extent to which information was available concerning an individual's relevant work performance) acted as a moderating variable. The results showed that acolytes initially benefited, in terms of promotions, from loose linkages between their unobservable quality and signals offered by their industry-leader ties, but also suffered, after initial promotions, in terms of fewer further promotions or lateral moves and more demotions, as the unreliability of social network signals became evident.

Sometimes, however, network measures are not summarized at the individual level. The data exhibit systematic dependence. For example, research examined whether 170 members of a Master's in Business Administration (MBA) class who were connected on one dimension, friendship, exhibited overlap on another dimension, namely, similarity in the organizations they interviewed with for jobs (Kilduff, 1992). The friendship and organizational similarity matrices contained 28,730 observations on all possible pairs of people. These observations were not independent of each other. Thus, the organizational similarity correlation between Chris and Carol was not independent of the organizational similarity correlation between Chris and Jack because both observations contained the same data from Chris. These kinds of data may exhibit autocorrelation that can generate biased estimations with ordinary-least-squares (OLS) tests.

A solution to the autocorrelation problem is the quadratic assignment procedure (QAP), which estimates the significance of a correlation between matrices, and the multiple regression-QAP (MRQAP), which estimates the significance of beta coefficients from regression analyses (Huber & Schultz, 1976; Krackhardt, 1988; e.g., Brands & Kilduff, 2014; Labianca et al., 2001; Pastor, Meindl, & Mayo, 2002). To estimate the significance of a correlation or a beta coefficient, these nonparametric procedures generate a reference distribution from the specific data that the researchers have collected. This involves repeatedly permuting rows and columns of one matrix (the dependent matrix for MRQAP) in the analysis while keeping the other matrix or matrices constant to generate a reference distribution of correlations or coefficients against which the observed value can be compared (Borgatti et al., 2018).

Exponential random graph models (ERGMs) also address analytical challenges arising from multiple dependencies in social network data (Daraganova & Robins, 2013), and allow researchers to model characteristics of networks, such as reciprocated ties and triads, as outcomes of explanatory factors. Organizational researchers (e.g., Lomi et al., 2014; Rank, Robins, & Pattison, 2010) increasingly use ERGMs to model tie formation. For example, building on ERGM analyses, Brennecke (2020) identified factors that explained the formation of dissonant ties in organizations, that is, connections with colleagues who are difficult but who can help solve work-related problems. Unlike QAP and MRQAP, which control away the network dependence, ERGMs model and interpret both structure and randomness in social networks, allowing researchers to specify the sources of dependence (Borgatti et al., 2018). They also allow researchers to investigate ties at multiple levels or across different networks (Wang, 2013).

Social networks are dynamic in nature. Recently, more research attention has been paid to the interplay between individuals' psychological processes and network change (Tasselli & Kilduff, 2021). This increasingly popular investigation focus has been facilitated by the development of analytical programs such as SIENA (Simulation Investigation for Empirical Network Analysis) (Ripley et al., 2022) based on the Stochastic Actor-Oriented Modeling (SAOM) approach (Snijders, 2001, 2005). This method allows researchers to examine how people's attributes, attitudes, and behaviors coevolve with structural features of social networks over time (Snijders, van de Bunt, & Steglich, 2010). So far, SIENA has been applied to organizational research on network changes (e.g., Schulte, Cohen, & Klein, 2012; Baker & Bulkley, 2014). For example, a study of social network position and turnover showed that people who thought more about quitting their jobs were likely to change their advice network and maintain their existing friendship network, although the change of networks did not affect people's turnover attitudes (Tröster et al., 2019).

The direction of causality is a problem in social network research even if data reflect network change. Network structure is not an exogenous variable (Borgatti & Halgin, 2011: 1178) but derives from actors' characteristics, behaviors, and actions; these, in turn, exert influence on opportunities for action. In some analytical approaches, a continuous network evolution is assumed (Snijders, 2005). Thus, the problem of endogeneity arises because "actors are not randomly assigned to positions" (Borgatti, Brass, & Halgin, 2014: 20). New statistical approaches (e.g., Snijders et al., 2010) help ameliorate this problem by modeling network and attribute change simultaneously. Alternatively, social network experiments can provide evidence in support of causality to supplement correlational studies (e.g., Iorio, 2022).

5 Current Debates

5.1 Agency and Structure: The Eternal Tension

Social network research currently strains to incorporate both the big data revolution involving networks with millions of nodes (e.g., Lee et al., 2010) and a new emphasis on purposeful action and the pursuit of advantage by individuals (e.g., Burt, 1992; Tasselli & Kilduff, 2021). With big data, there is excitement over the possibility of examining the properties of very large networks as they evolve and change. Researchers in this tradition examine common features across heterogeneous networks including biological networks, cocitation networks, and the World Wide Web (e.g., Dorogovtsev & Mendes, 2003). The emphasis is on examining the ways in which clusters develop, the processes by which highly connected actors develop even more connections (e.g., Newman, 2002), and the extent to which networks exhibit resilience to attack (e.g., Moore & Westley, 2011). Key questions in this structural configuration research include: How do structural features such as large components featuring millions of connected nodes affect flows across the network? And does the network resemble a small world (i.e., a network characterized by a high degree of clustering together with short paths between any two actors – Uzzi & Spiro, 2005)?

On the side of individual agency, the publication of Burt's (1992) *Structural Holes* book, with its description of the *tertius gaudens* broker who spans across gaps in the social structure, brought a new focus on the ways in which people use social connections for advantage. In this world of competitive action between individuals, agency is ever-present: "The tertius plays conflicting demands and preferences against one another and builds value from their disunion" (Burt, 1992: 34).

A contrasting agentic approach is represented by the *tertius iungens* broker, the third who joins others to create collaboration among those who might not otherwise engage in work projects (Obstfeld, 2005). The *tertius iungens* research emphasis is on the *process* of bringing people into collaborative endeavors rather than on the *structure* of advantage that was emphasized in some prior brokerage research (Obstfeld, Borgatti, & Davis, 2014).

The big data and agentic approaches to social networks pull against each other. The big data emphasis draws on the structural foundations of social network research to capture the lineaments of giant webs of interconnections, whereas the research on individual agency sees the structure of social networks as representing opportunities for individual actors to gain advantage through systems of relationships that can be forged, bridged, and broken (Burt, Kilduff, & Tasselli, 2013).

Thus, structure and agency represent two ways of looking at social networks. In examining the structure of a network, the focus is on the overall pattern of ties at different levels of analysis. At the individual ego-network level, structure concerns whether the people to whom the individual is tied, that is, the alters, are themselves connected to each other (e.g., Oh & Kilduff, 2008). At the level of whole networks, structure is examined in terms of whether there is evidence of a core/periphery structure (e.g., Cattani & Ferriani, 2008), or whether networks exhibit small-worldness (e.g., Kilduff et al., 2008).

These structural emphases neglect the question of whether and how agentic actors create, reproduce, and transform social structures in their own interests (Emirbayer & Mische, 1998). Change in social networks from an agentic perspective is prompted by motivated people in pursuit of outcomes that are important at the collective (e.g., Obstfeld, 2005) or at the individual level where social ties can be regarded as investments "in social relations with expected returns in the market-place" (Lin, 2001: 19).

The tension between agency and structure involves a dualism between individuality, representative of the "push" factor of motivation from within, and social networks, representative of the "pull" factor of structures of opportunity from without. Models of social action that incorporate both the motivations and capabilities of individuals and the constraints and opportunities provided by network structures are available (e.g., Tasselli et al., 2015) but are difficult to incorporate within a single study.

5.2 Network Volatility

Social network research has tended to privilege stability rather than change, with just 11 percent of social network papers published in the last two decades explicitly assessing network dynamics (for a recent review, see Chen et al., 2022). The argument for more research on dynamics is that network volatility is intrinsic in network research. Social networks are complex adaptive systems constituted both by established structures of relationships and by evolving patterns of expectations and perceptions (Kilduff et al., 2006). But many relationships, such as friendship, tend to be relatively stable, as one study of MBA students' friendships observed: "Over the time period studied there was no significant change in homophily among the racial groups' networks, despite the explicit promotion of diversity in recruitment of students, formation of heterogeneous classes and teams, and active support by the MBA program administrators" (Mollica, Gray, & Trevino, 2003: 123).

Early work by Barnard argued that people in social contexts attract and repel each other like "components in a magnetic field" (Barnard, 1938: 75). The idea of repulsion and attraction, in terms of both homophily and propinquity, was also inherent in most foundational work on the dynamics of network relations. Newcomb (1961) observed the "acquaintance process" of initial strangers – "seventeen men who were transferring from other institutions of higher learning to the University of Michigan" (Newcomb, 1961: 2) – during the period of development and stabilization of their relationships. According to Newcomb's analysis, reciprocated relationships among strangers tended to stabilize over a period of about three weeks. But a closer examination of those results suggested a different view, showing that reciprocity often tended to fluctuate and some individuals "danced between friends" over the entire observation period of fifteen weeks (Moody et al., 2005: 1229).

Other famous foundational studies combined ethnographic inquiry and a network approach in investigating the evolution of network structures over time, including the "karate club" study conducted by Zachary (1977), which analyzed the structure of relationships in a karate club before and after its split into two different clubs. Due to the ideological conflict between the club president and the club instructor over both the price of karate lessons and the type of karate being practiced, the club was differentiated before the split in two highly centralized blocks around the two actors. Over time, these opposite pressures led the club to divide into two distinct clubs following the two leaders. Through the use of block modelling and sociograms,

Zachary's analysis suggests that a network aimed at achieving a goal will, in the presence of goal conflict, tend to form two groups differentiated on the basis of different goals.

A later approach to volatility emphasized the role of "shocks" in providing opportunities for actors to restructure their ties. External shocks can include technological change (Barley, 1990; Sasovova et al., 2010) and industrial action (Meyer, 1982), whereas internal shocks can include the potential distortive effects of new management (Burt & Ronchi, 1990). Shocks can increase the degree of uncertainty experienced by individual actors, with efforts to reduce uncertainty resulting in a change of communication patterns between individuals and groups (e.g., Barley, 1990).

More recent studies have addressed theoretical issues underlying patterns of volatility and stability inherent in network dynamics, with emphasis given to temporal antecedents and consequences of brokerage dynamics (e.g., Burt & Merluzzi, 2016). In a study using four years of data on the social networks of bankers in a large organization, interpersonal bridges relative to other kinds of relationships showed faster rates of decay over time (Burt, 2002), with nine out of ten bridges vanishing in the average period of a year. A more detailed analysis of these results, however, showed that decay varied according to an actor's experience in managing structural holes: slower decay was found in the networks of bankers experienced with bridge relationships, suggesting that social capital tends to accrue to those who already have it.

Dispositional forces, such as the individual's personality, contribute to the churning of interpersonal connections such that "individuals help (re)create the social network structures they inhabit" (Sasovova et al., 2010: 639). The social structures that individuals forge tend to maintain an overall inertia over time, even as the connections underlying those structures are shaped by the happenstance of individual choices and external events (Moody et al., 2005).

Overall, volatility and stability in network connections represent a duality characteristic of "boundedly rational actors creating and re-creating the social structures within which their opportunities and constraints evolve" (Kilduff et al., 2006: 1038). We lack evidence, however, on the advantages and disadvantages associated with the different degrees of volatility (and stability) that individuals experience in their networks of connections. Volatility can enhance opportunities for network advantage (Burt, 2002). But volatility can also imperil individuals' career prospects in cases where the legitimacy necessary for the adding and cutting of relationships is absent (Burt, 1992).

The research on network dynamics employs its own vocabulary and methods, as summarized in the glossary provided in Table 4.

Table 4 Glossary of terms related to social network dynamics.

Term	Description
Churn	This connotes continual change (e.g., Sasovova et al., 2010) and is often applied to changes in a node's ego network (e.g., Siciliano, Welch, & Feeney, 2018).
Network trajectories	Primarily used in the context of nodes, it refers to change in the composition of ties, or in the node's social capital (e.g., Kilduff & Tsai, 2003). Another use is describing the pattern of change of a whole network over time, for example the trajectories of one network becoming more cohesive; another becoming more decentralized (Borgatti et al., 2002).
Network patterns	These relate to the stratification of network structures and configurations in a given social system. Over time, network patterns define the social space of a given system (e.g., Burt, 1982).
Endogenous network change	This is used to describe changes in the network that can be modeled without data on node characteristics (e.g., gender or age) or without other kinds of tie (e.g., friendship when studying advice) (e.g., Amati, Lomi, & Mira, 2018). In other contexts, it refers to change caused by factors internal to a group, such as a team or an organization (e.g., Lomi et al., 2014).
Exogenous network change	It describes changes in the network generated by or associated with an external jolt (e.g., the introduction of a new technology in the organization – Sasovova et al., 2010).
Network equilibrium	This is a state in which forces of change counteract each other such that network patterns stay the same even though some ties may be in flux (e.g., Moody et al., 2005).
Network evolution	This refers to a process of network emergence, formation, reconfiguration, decay, and dissolution (e.g., Burt, 2002; Zheng et al., 2019).
Network oscillation	It is a pattern of network change characterized by periods of activity and periods of stability. For example, effective brokers oscillate between

Table 4 (cont.)

Term	Description
	periods of spanning across structural holes and retreating within closed networks (Burt & Merluzzi 2016).
Network orchestration/ governance	This describes activities performed by central actors in the network to coordinate, influence, and direct other actors (e.g., Heidl, Steensma, & Phelps, 2014; Nambisan & Sawhney, 2011).
Network multiplexity	It relates to the presence of multiple types of relationship between the same actors (Shipilov et al., 2014: 450) at interpersonal and intra- and interorganizational levels. For example, two firms have a multiplex tie if they are connected by a board interlock and a strategic alliance (Sytch & Tatarynowicz, 2014). At the individual level, it can describe the presence of different relationships between two people, such as friendship and advice-giving (Clarke et al., 2021). Recent research examined the dynamics of temporal multiplexity, that is, the overlaying of ties of different duration (Operti, Lampronti, & Sgourev, 2020).
Network dynamics	This umbrella term incorporates concepts ranging from network change to the occurrence of relational events, influence, and flows (e.g., Ahuja, Soda, & Zaheer, 2012).
Network change	This term defines change in (a) dyadic states or (b) higher-order constructs such as centralization. It can also define (c) changes in whole-network properties, such as density. Like "network dynamics," it is also used to reference changes happening at the network level over time (e.g., Kim, Oh, & Swaminathan, 2006).
Network stability	It can define lack of change or patterns of stasis before or after patterns of change. A network is described as stable if it does not change (e.g., Oh & Jeon, 2007), but a network can also be described as stable if it is experiencing a moment of stasis

Table 4 (cont.)

Term	Description
	between periods of change (e.g., Burt & Merluzzi, 2016).
MRQAP	In cases where network data exhibit systematic autocorrelation, this procedure (multiple regression-QAP) generates a reference distribution from the data against which regression coefficients can be assessed for significance (e.g., Kilduff & Krackhardt, 1994).
ERGMs	These procedures (exponential random graph models) model the interdependences between different types of network tie. Specifically, they model the probability that a tie from i to j exists as a function of predictors, where each predictor corresponds to an actor-specific factor or a local configuration of ties (e.g., Robins, Pattison, & Wang, 2009; Snijders et al., 2006). The ERGMs family also includes MERGMs (multilevel exponential random graph models), a class of logit models for network data (Wang et al., 2013), and STERGMs (separable temporal exponential random graph models), which account for longitudinal change in network relational structures, testing the probability of a new tie forming over time (e.g., Krivitsky & Handcock, 2014).

5.3 Boundaries of Social Networks

Social network research has long focused on the advantages, constraints, and actions of focal individuals. Neglected in this focus have been the alters to whom individuals are connected. An alter-focused research endeavor has begun, however, with examination of ways in which alters affect ego's centrality (e.g., Tasselli, Neray, & Lomi, 2023) or brokerage (e.g., Kleinbaum et al., 2015). But the question arises of where to draw the boundary delineating possible influence on the individual. Should the boundary be restricted to individuals' direct contacts, or should it be extended to include indirect contacts of individuals' actors (i.e., the direct contacts of their contacts)? Research is conflicted on this question. Economic outcomes in organizations may be affected only by the set of direct contacts around the individual (Burt, 2007), but this remains true only if the indirect ties of high-ranking colleagues are neglected (Galunic et al., 2012).

The question of whether to include indirect connections in network research is relevant because longitudinal studies conducted in a variety of settings find significant effects linking direct and indirect ties to propensity to suffer from obesity, smoking cessation (Christakis & Fowler, 2007), happiness in the workplace (Fowler & Christakis, 2008), and social status and prestige (Lin et al., 1981). As yet unanswered are the effects of direct and indirect ties in relationships that are negative (Labianca & Brass, 2006), conflictual (Klein et al., 2004), or emotional (Menges & Kilduff, 2015). To what extent are people affected by experiences, cognitions, and feelings that are several connections removed?

These questions have particular urgency for the growing area of social network interventions designed to improve intraorganizational functioning by identifying coalitions and analyzing intergroup relations (Nelson, 1988), and at the macro level to improve health outcomes, disseminate innovations, and make organizations more effective (Valente, 2012). Social network research has matured sufficiently for its ideas and technologies to be substantially useful in practice.

5.4 Personality and Networks

Is network change driven by individual action, structural embeddedness, or the coevolution of individual characteristics and behaviors and the properties of network interactions (Tasselli et al., 2015)? Currently, we lack research that examines the dynamic patterns connecting individual identity and network configuration. Although personality variables have been treated by microfoundational network research as independent (and immutable) predictors of network change (e.g., Sasovova et al., 2010), future work can investigate the possibility that the individual's personality itself changes as he or she experiences changing network positions. New research shows that relationship experiences, such as friendship and kinship, affect personality development (Mund & Neyer, 2014). Previously, the discovery that personality in the form of self-monitoring influenced the occupation of advantageous network positions (e.g., Mehra et al., 2001; Sasovova et al., 2010) challenged the structural hegemony of network research (Mayhew, 1980). Now, the challenge is to build on the volume of work that shows the mutability of personality (Tasselli, Kilduff, & Landis, 2018) to gauge the extent to which individuals change their dispositions in response to social network opportunities and constraints.

6 Future Research

6.1 Brokerage as Individual Advantage and Community Contribution

An individual view of agency (e.g., Lin, 2001) emphasizes individual achievement through network connections, whereas the embeddedness tradition (e.g., Granovetter, 1973. 1985) focuses on social structure constraints and facilitation. These views compete on whether people or networks fuel social action. This tension is both reflected in and intrinsic to social network theory, but also gives opportunities for integration of competing views. Structural-hole theory (Burt, 1992, 1997), for example, depicts brokerage as a highly agentic activity in which people negotiate between the "pulsing swirl of mixed, conflicting demands" for their own advantage (Burt, 1992: 33). Brokers are seen as network entrepreneurs who enable change (Burt et al., 1998). At the same time, structural-hole theory suggests that achievement accrues to those who provide value to the community of interacting participants by supplying good ideas (Burt, 2004), mentoring junior colleagues (Burt, 1992), and performing distinctive work (Burt, 1997). There is increasing interest in taking alter-centered approaches rather than continuing to focus on advantages accruing to the broker (Brass, 2022). Thus, there is an opportunity to bridge between the individual advantage and the embeddedness approaches. Indeed, recent work indicates that successful social network brokers are those who engage in "punctuated brokerage," a pattern of interaction that features intermittent brokering with periods in which the broker retreats within a closed, rather than an open, network structure (Burt & Merluzzi, 2016).

6.2 Network Cognition: From Bias to Opportunity

Implicit in the work on network cognition is the assumption that accurate perceptions of networks are advantageous in terms of future interactions and organizational outcomes (e.g., Brands, 2013: S93). Network accuracy is seen as helping individuals scan the map of their social world in search of opportunities and advantage (e.g., Krackhardt, 1990). The alternative possibility is that misalignments in network perceptions are leading indicators of network change. Rather than seeking to correct individuals' mistaken network perceptions, therefore, as prescribed in prior research and practitioner advice (e.g., Krackhardt & Hanson, 1993), individuals can be made aware of the possibility that environments can be enacted through purposeful efforts, so that actual relationships can catch up with perceptions.

Network misalignment, therefore, could be recategorized as a form of cognitive social capital that has the potential to be converted into actual social capital.

6.3 Past Ties

Research on ties that span temporal configurations suggests that it is not only current social capital that helps facilitate individuals' outcomes. Dormant ties (originated in the past and reestablished in the present) – that is, "former ties, now out of touch" – are repositories of vital and accessible help (Levin, Walter, & Murnighan, 2011: 923). Given this, we envisage research aimed at analyzing the effects on present interactions of the legacy of past relationships. People forge and change ties in the present, but their actions may be embedded in networks of past ties, also referred to as "ghost ties" (Kilduff et al., 2006). Research on network memory shows the temporal effects of structural holes and closure on performance (e.g., Soda, Usai, & Zaheer, 2004). Future research is needed to investigate the often-hidden influence of prior social network ties, both positive and negative, on current networking patterns.

7 Conclusion

We have introduced and discussed key elements that drive the organizational social networks research program, including its historical foundations, distinctive ideas and theories, epistemological approaches and methods, current debates, and future directions. Our contributions are threefold. First, we promote critical discussion of the core ideas and debates at the heart of the social networks research field. Organizational social network research, in our view, maintains theoretical and methodological consistency in answering questions that include: How do people forge and shape ties in organizations? How do network properties and structures emerging from these interaction patterns explain individual and organizational outcomes? We have discussed theories and methods that help researchers answer these questions. Simultaneously, we are conscious that the social networks research program continues to evolve as it extends its generative capabilities.

Social network research is exemplary, in our view, in bridging micro and macro perspectives, bringing attention not only to how individual differences contribute to structural patterning but also to how the structure of networks influences individual actions and identities. From our perspective, the tension between individual agency and network structure continues to drive research opportunities of relevance to people's careers and lives. People generate and change over time the social network structures in which they live and work, and these structures affect, in turn, the way people, individually and collectively, think and behave. As an evolving research program, social network research combines both the intellectual vitality and the methodological flexibility required to tackle leading questions concerning individuals and organizations in the flux of transformation.

References

Abolafia, M. Y. & Kilduff, M. (1988). Enacting market crisis: The social construction of a speculative bubble. *Administrative Science Quarterly*, **33**(2), 177–193.

Adler, P. S. & Kwon, S. W. (2002). Social capital: Prospects for a new concept. *Academy of Management Review*, **27**(1), 17–40.

Agneessens, F. & Labianca, G. J. (2022). Collecting survey-based social network information in work organizations. *Social Networks*, **68** (1), 31–47.

Ahuja, G., Soda, G. & Zaheer, A. (2012). The genesis and dynamics of organizational networks. *Organization Science*, **23**(2), 434–448.

Amati, V., Lomi, A. & Mira, A. (2018). Social network modeling. *Annual Review of Statistics and Its Application*, **5**, 343–369.

Arthur, M. B. & Rousseau, D. M. (1996). *The Boundaryless Career*. New York: Oxford University Press.

Baer, M. (2010). The strength-of-weak-ties perspective on creativity: A comprehensive examination and extension. *Journal of Applied Psychology*, **95**(3), 592–601.

Baker, W. E. (1984). The social structure of a national securities market. *American Journal of Sociology*, **89**(4), 775–811.

Baker, W. E. & Bulkley, N. (2014). Paying it forward vs. rewarding reputation: Mechanisms of generalized reciprocity. *Organization Science*, **25**(5), 1493–1510.

Balkundi, P. & Harrison, D. A. (2006). Ties, leaders, and time in teams: Strong inference about network structure's effects on team viability and performance. *Academy of Management Journal*, **49**(1), 49–68.

Barley, S. R. (1990). The alignment of technology and structure through roles and networks. *Administrative Science Quarterly*, **35**(1), 61–103.

Barnard, C. (1938). *The Functions of the Executive*. Cambridge, MA: Harvard University Press.

Battilana, J. & Casciaro, T. (2012). Change agents, networks, and institutions: A contingency theory of organizational change. *Academy of Management Journal*, **55**(2), 381–398.

Baum, J. A. C., Shipilov, A. V. & Rowley, T. J. (2003). Where do small worlds come from? *Industrial and Corporate Change*, **12**(4), 697–725.

Berkman, L. F. & Syme, S. L. (1979). Social networks, host resistance, and mortality: A nine-year follow-up study of Alameda County residents. *American Journal of Epidemiology*, **109**(2), 186–204.

Biernacki, P. & Waldorf, D. (1981). Snowball sampling: Problems and techniques of chain referral sampling. *Sociological Methods & Research*, **10**(2), 141–163.

Blau, P. M. (1977). A macrosociological theory of social structure. *American Journal of Sociology*, **83**(1), 26–54.

Blau, P. M., Blum, T. C. & Schwartz, J. E. (1982). Heterogeneity and intermarriage. *American Sociological Review*, **47**(1), 45–62.

Bonacich, P. (1972). Factoring and weighting approaches to clique identification. *Journal of Mathematical Sociology*, **2**(1), 113–120.

(2007). Some unique properties of eigenvector centrality. *Social Networks*, **29**(4), 555–564.

Boorman, S. A. & White, H. C. (1976). Social structure from multiple networks. II. Role structures. *American Journal of Sociology*, **81**(6), 1384–1446.

Borgatti, S. P. (2005). Centrality and network flow. *Social Networks*, **27**(1), 55–71.

Borgatti, S. P. & Everett, M. G. (2000). Models of core/periphery structures. *Social Networks*, **21**(4), 375–395.

(2006). A graph-theoretic perspective on centrality. *Social Networks*, **28**(4), 466–484.

Borgatti, S. P. & Halgin, D. S. (2011). On network theory. *Organization Science*, **22**(5), 1168–1181.

Borgatti, S. P., Brass, D. J. & Halgin, D. S. (2014). Social network research: Confusions, criticisms, and controversies. *Research in the Sociology of Organizations*, **40**, 1–29.

Borgatti, S. P., Carley, K. M. & Krackhardt, D. (2006). On the robustness of centrality measures under conditions of imperfect data. *Social Networks*, **28**(2), 124–136.

Borgatti, S. P., Everett, M. G. & Freeman, L. C. (1999). *UCINET 5 for Windows*. Columbia, SC: Analytic Technologies.

(2002). *UCINET for Windows: Software for Social Network Analysis*. Harvard, MA: Analytic Technologies.

Borgatti, S. P., Everett, M. G. & Johnson, J. C. (2013). *Analyzing Social Networks*. London: Sage.

(2018). *Analyzing Social Networks*, 2nd ed. London: Sage.

Borgatti, S. P., Jones, C. & Everett, M. G. (1998). Network measures of social capital. *Connections*, **21**(2), 27–36.

Bott, E. (1955). Urban families, conjugal roles and social networks. *Human Relations*, **8**(4), 345–383.

Brands, R. A. (2013). Cognitive social structures in social network research: A review. *Journal of Organizational Behavior*, **34**(S1), S82–S103.

Brands, R. A. & Kilduff, M. (2014). Just like a woman? Effects of gender-biased perceptions of friendship network brokerage on attributions and performance. *Organization Science*, **25**(5), 1530–1548.

Brands, R. A. & Mehra, A. (2019). Gender, brokerage, and performance: A construal approach. *Academy of Management Journal*, **62**(1), 196–219.

Brass, D. J. (1984). Being in the right place: A structural analysis of individual influence in an organization. *Administrative Science Quarterly*, **29**(4), 518–539.

(2022). New developments in social network analysis. *Annual Review of Organizational Psychology and Organizational Behavior*, **9**, 225–246.

Breiger, R. L. (1974). The duality of persons and groups. *Social Forces*, **53**(2), 181–190.

Brennecke, J. (2020). Dissonant ties in intraorganizational networks: Why individuals seek problem-solving assistance from difficult colleagues. *Academy of Management Journal*, **63**(3), 743–778.

Burt, R. S. (1980). Autonomy in a social topology. *American Journal of Sociology*, **85**(4), 892–925.

(1982). *Toward a Structural Theory of Action*. New York: Academic Press.

(1984). Network items and the general social survey. *Social Networks*, **6**(4), 293–340.

(1987). Social contagion and innovation: Cohesion versus structural equivalence. *American Journal of Sociology*, **92**(6), 1287–1335.

(1992). *Structural Holes: The Social Structure of Competition*. Cambridge, MA: Harvard University Press.

(1997). The contingent value of social capital. *Administrative Science Quarterly*, **42**(2), 339–365.

(1998). The gender of social capital. *Rationality and Society*, **10**(1), 5–46.

(2000). The network structure of social capital. *Research in Organizational Behavior*, **22**, 345–423.

(2002). Bridge decay. *Social Networks*, **24**(4), 333–363.

(2004). Structural holes and good ideas. *American Journal of Sociology*, **110**(2), 349–399.

(2005). *Brokerage and Closure: An Introduction to Social Capital*. Oxford: Oxford University Press.

(2007). Secondhand brokerage: Evidence on the importance of local structure for managers, bankers, and analysts. *Academy of Management Journal*, **50**(1), 119–148.

(2010). *Neighbor Networks: Competitive Advantage Local and Personal*. Oxford: Oxford University Press.

(2012). Network-related personality and the agency question: Multi-role evidence from a virtual world. *American Journal of Sociology*, **118**(3), 543–591.

(2021). Structural holes capstone, cautions, and enthusiasms. In M. L. Small, B. L. Perry, B. Pescosolido, & N. Smith, eds., *Personal Networks: Classic Readings and New Directions in Egocentric Analysis*. New York: Cambridge University Press.

Burt, R. S. & Lin, N. (1977). Network time series from archival records. *Sociological Methodology*, **8**, 224–254.

Burt, R. S. & Merluzzi, J. (2016). Network oscillation. *Academy of Management Discoveries*, **2**(4), 368–391.

Burt, R. S. & Ronchi, D. (1990). Contested control in a large manufacturing plant. In J. Wessie & H. Flap, eds., *Social Networks Through Time*. Utrecht: ISOR, pp. 121–157.

Burt, R. S. & Wang, S. (2021). Bridge supervision: Correlates of a boss on the far side of a structural hole. *Academy of Management Journal*, **65**(6), 1835–1863.

Burt, R. S., Jannotta, J. E. & Mahoney, J. T. (1998). Personality correlates of structural holes. *Social Networks*, **20**(1), 63–87.

Burt, R. S., Kilduff, M. & Tasselli, S. (2013). Social network analysis: Foundations and frontiers on advantage. *Annual Review of Psychology*, **64**, 527–547.

Buskens, V. & van de Rijt, A. (2008). Dynamics of networks if everyone strives for structural holes. *American Journal of Sociology*, **114**(2), 371–407.

Cacioppo, J. T., Fowler, J. H. & Christakis, N. A. (2009). Alone in the crowd: The structure and spread of loneliness in a large social network. *Journal of Personality and Social Psychology*, **97**(6), 977–991.

Carley, K. (1991). A theory of group stability. *American Sociological Review*, **56**(3), 331–354.

Cartwright, D. & Harary, F. (1956). Structural balance: A generalization of Heider's theory. *Psychological Review*, **63**(5), 277–293.

Cartwright, N. (1983). *How the Laws of Physics Lie*. Oxford: Clarendon Press.

Casciaro, T., Gino, F. & Kouchaki, M. (2014). The contaminating effects of building instrumental ties: How networking can make us feel dirty. *Administrative Science Quarterly*, **59**(4), 705–735.

Cattani, G. & Ferriani, S. (2008). A core/periphery perspective on individual creative performance: Social networks and cinematic achievements in the Hollywood film industry. *Organization Science*, **19**(6), 824–844.

Centola, D. & Macy, M. (2007). Complex contagions and the weakness of long ties. *American Journal of Sociology*, **113**(3), 702–734.

Chen, H., Mehra, A., Tasselli, S. & Borgatti, S. P. (2022). Network dynamics and organizations: A review and research agenda. *Journal of Management,* **48**(6), 1602–1660.

Christakis, N. A. & Fowler, J. H. (2007). The spread of obesity in a large social network over 32 years. *New England Journal of Medicine,* **357**(4), 370–379.

Chua, R. Y., Morris, M. W. & Ingram, P. (2009). Guanxi vs networking: Distinctive configurations of affect-and cognition-based trust in the networks of Chinese vs American managers. *Journal of International Business Studies,* **40**(3), 490–508.

Chung, M. H., Park, J., Moon, H. K. & Oh, H. (2011). The multilevel effects of network embeddedness on interpersonal citizenship behavior. *Small Group Research,* **42**(6), 730–760.

Chung, Y. & Jackson, S. E. (2013). The internal and external networks of knowledge-intensive teams: The role of task routineness. *Journal of Management,* **39**(2), 442–468.

Clarke, R., Richter, A. W. & Kilduff, M. (2021). One tie to capture advice and friendship: Leader multiplex centrality effects on team performance change. *Journal of Applied Psychology,* **107**(6), 968–986.

Cohen, S. & Janicki-Deverts, D. (2009). Can we improve our physical health by altering our social networks? *Perspectives on Psychological Science,* **4**(4), 375–378.

Cohen, S., Doyle, W. J., Skoner, D. P., Rabin, B. S. & Gwaltney, J. M. (1997). Social ties and susceptibility to the common cold. *Jama,* **277**(24), 1940–1944.

Coleman, J. S. (1988). Social capital in the creation of human capital. *American Journal of Sociology,* **94**, S95–S120.

(1990). *Foundations of Social Theory.* Cambridge, MA: Harvard University Press.

Coleman, J. S., Katz, E. & Menzel, H. (1966). *Medical Innovation.* New York: Bobbs-Merrill.

Cross, R. & Cummings, J. N. (2004). Tie and network correlates of individual performance in knowledge-intensive work. *Academy of Management Journal,* **47**(6), 928–937.

Cross, R., Borgatti, S. P. & Parker, A. (2002). Making invisible work visible: Using social network analysis to support strategic collaboration. *California Management Review,* **44**(2), 25–46.

Cuypers, I. R., Ertug, G., Cantwell, J., Zaheer, A. & Kilduff, M. (2020). Making connections: Social networks in international business. *Journal of International Business Studies,* **51**(5), 714–736.

Daraganova, G. & Robins, G. (2013). Autologistic actor attribute models. In D. Lusher, J. Koskinen & G. Robins, eds., *Exponential Random Graph Models for Social Networks: Theory, Methods, and Applications*. New York: Cambridge University Press, pp. 102–114.

Davis, A., Gardner, B. B. & Gardner, M. R. (1941). *Deep South: A Social Anthropological Study of Caste and Class*. Chicago, IL: University of Chicago Press.

Davis, G. F. (1991). Agents without principles? The spread of the poison pill through the intercorporate network. *Administrative Science Quarterly*, **36**(4), 583–613.

Davis, G. F. & Greve, H. R. (1997). Corporate elite networks and governance changes in the 1980s. *American Journal of Sociology*, **103**(1), 1–37.

DiMaggio, P. (1986). Structural analysis of organizational fields: A blockmodel approach. *Research in Organizational Behavior*, **8**, 335–370.

Direnzo, M. S. & Greenhaus, J. H. (2011). Job search and voluntary turnover in a boundaryless world: A control theory perspective. *Academy of Management Review*, **36**(3), 567–589.

Dodds, P. S., Muhamad, R. & Watts, D. J. (2003). An experimental study of search in global social networks. *Science*, **301**(5634), 827–829.

Doreian, P. & Mrvar, A. (2009). Partitioning signed social networks. *Social Networks*, **31**(1), 1–11.

Dorogovtsev, S. N. & Mendes, J. F. (2003). *Evolution of Networks: From Biological Nets to the Internet and WWW*. Oxford: Oxford University Press.

Durkheim, É. (1951). *Suicide*. New York: Free Press.

Ellis, P. D. (2011). Social ties and international entrepreneurship: Opportunities and constraints affecting firm internationalization. *Journal of International Business Studies*, **42**(1), 99–127.

Emirbayer, M. & Goodwin, J. (1994). Network analysis, culture, and the problem of agency. *American Journal of Sociology*, **99**(6), 1411–1454.

Emirbayer, M. & Mische, A. (1998). What is agency? *American Journal of Sociology*, **103**(4), 962–1023.

Erickson, B. (1988). The relational basis of attitudes. In B. Wellman & S. Berkowitz, eds., *Social Structures: A Network Approach*. New York: Cambridge University Press, pp. 99–121.

Faris, R., Felmlee, D. & McMillan, C. (2020). With friends like these: Aggression from amity and equivalence. *American Journal of Sociology*, **126**(3), 673–713.

Fernandez, R. M. (2021). Strength in weak ties in the labor market: An assessment of the state of research. In M. L. Small, B. L. Perry, B. A. Pescosolido

& E. B. Smith, eds., *Personal Networks: Classic Readings and New Directions in Egocentric Analysis.* Cambridge: Cambridge University Press, pp. 251–264.

Fernandez, R. M. & Gould, R. V. (1994). A dilemma of state power: Brokerage and influence in the national health policy domain. *American Journal of Sociology*, **99**(6), 1455–1491.

Fernandez, R. M., Castilla, E. J. & Moore, P. (2000). Social capital at work: Networks and employment at a phone center. *American Journal of Sociology*, **105**(5), 1288–1356.

Flynn, F. J., Reagans, R. E., Amanatullah, E. T. & Ames, D. R. (2006). Helping one's way to the top: Self-monitors achieve status by helping others and knowing who helps whom. *Journal of Personality and Social Psychology*, **91**(6), 1123–1137.

Fowler, J. H. & Christakis, N. A. (2008). Dynamic spread of happiness in a large social network: Longitudinal analysis over 20 years in the Framingham Heart Study. *British Medical Journal*, **338**, a2338.

Frank, O. (1978). Sampling and estimation in large social networks. *Social Networks*, **1**(1), 91–101.

(1979). Estimating a graph from triad counts. *Journal of Statistical Computation and Simulation*, **9**(1), 31–46.

Freeman, L. C. (1977). A set of measures of centrality based on betweenness. *Sociometry*, **40**(1), 35–41.

(1979). Centrality in social networks: Conceptual clarification. *Social Networks*, **1**(3), 215–239.

(2004). *The Development of Social Network Analysis: A Study in the Sociology of Science.* Vancouver: Empirical Press.

Freeman, L. C., Roeder, D. & Mulholland, R. R. (1979). Centrality in social networks: II. Experimental results. *Social Networks*, **2**(2), 119–141.

Freeman, L. C., Romney, A. K. & Freeman, S. C. (1987). Cognitive structure and informant accuracy. *American Anthropologist*, **89**(2), 310–325.

Friedman, M. (1953). *Essays in Positive Economics.* Chicago, IL: University of Chicago Press.

Fukuyama, F. (2002). Social capital and development. *SAIS Review*, **22**, 23–37.

Furnari, S. (2014). Interstitial spaces: Microinteraction settings and the genesis of new practices between institutional fields. *Academy of Management Review*, **39**(4), 439–462.

Galunic, C., Ertug, G. & Gargiulo, M. (2012). The positive externalities of social capital: Benefiting from senior brokers. *Academy of Management Journal*, **55**(5), 1213–1231.

Ghoshal, S. & Bartlett, C. A. (1990). The multinational corporation as an inter-organizational network. *Academy of Management Review*, **15**(4), 603–626.

Goffman, E. (1969). *Strategic Interaction*. Philadelphia: University of Pennsylvania Press.

Goyal, S. (2007). *Connections: An Introduction to the Economics of Networks*. Princeton, NJ: Princeton University Press.

Granovetter, M. S. (1973). The strength of weak ties. *American Journal of Sociology*, **78**(6), 1360–1380.

(1983). The strength of weak ties: A network theory revisited. *Sociological Theory*, **1**, 201–233.

(1985). Economic action and social structure: The problem of embeddedness. *American Journal of Sociology*, **91**(3), 481–510.

(2005). The impact of social structure on economic outcomes. *Journal of Economic Perspectives*, **19**(1), 33–50.

Gulati, R., Nohria, N. & Zaheer, A. (2000). Strategic networks. *Strategic Management Journal*, **21**(3), 203–215.

Halevy, N. & Kalish, Y. (2021). Broadening versus deepening: Gender and brokering in social networks. *Social Psychological and Personality Science*, **13**(2), 618–625.

Hansen, M. T. (1999). The search-transfer problem: The role of weak ties in sharing knowledge across organization subunits. *Administrative Science Quarterly*, **44**(1), 82–111.

Harary, F., Norman, R. & Cartwright, D. (1965). *Structural Models*. New York: Wiley.

Hargadon, A. B. (2006). Bridging old worlds and building new ones: Towards a microsociology of creativity. In L. Thompson & H. S. Choi, eds., *Creativity and Innovation in Organizational Teams*. London: Lawrence Erlbaum Associates, pp. 199–216.

Hayton, J. C., Carnabuci, G. & Eisenberger, R. (2012). With a little help from my colleagues: A social embeddedness approach to perceived organizational support. *Journal of Organizational Behavior*, **33**(2), 235–249.

Heider, F. (1946). Attitudes and cognitive organization. *Journal of Psychology*, **21**(1), 107–112.

(1958). *The Psychology of Interpersonal Relations*. Hoboken, NJ: Wiley.

Heidl, R. A., Steensma, H. K. & Phelps, C. (2014). Divisive faultlines and the unplanned dissolutions of multipartner alliances. *Organization Science*, **25**(5), 1351–1371.

Holland, P. W. & Leinhardt, S. (1977). Transitivity in structural models of small groups. In S. Leinhardt, ed., *Social Networks: A Developing Paradigm*. New York: Academic Press, pp. 49–66.

Huber, L. J. & Schultz, J. (1976). Quadratic assignment as a general data analysis strategy. *British Journal of Mathematical and Statistical Psychology*, **29**(2), 190–241.

Hummon, N. P. & Carley, K. (1993). Social networks as normal science. *Social Networks*, **15**(1), 71–106.

Ingram, P. & Morris, M. W. (2007). Do people mix at mixers? Structure, homophily, and the "life of the party." *Administrative Science Quarterly*, **52**(4), 558–585.

Iorio, A. (2022). Brokers in disguise: The joint effect of actual brokerage and socially perceived brokerage on network advantage. *Administrative Science Quarterly*, **67**(3), 769–820.

Janicik, G. A. & Larrick, R. P. (2005). Social network schemas and the learning of incomplete networks. *Journal of Personality and Social Psychology*, **88**(2), 348–364.

Jensen, M. & Wang, P. (2018). Not in the same boat: How status inconsistency affects research performance in business schools. *Academy of Management Journal*, **61**(3), 1021–1049.

Kapferer, B. (1972). *Strategy and Transaction in an African Factory: African Workers and Indian Management in a Zambian Town*. Manchester: Manchester University Press.

Kilduff, G. J. (2019). Interfirm relational rivalry: Implications for competitive strategy. *Academy of Management Review*, **44**(4), 775–799.

Kilduff, M. (1992). The friendship network as a decision-making resource: Dispositional moderators of social influences on organizational choice. *Journal of Personality and Social Psychology*, **62**(1), 168–180.

Kilduff, M. & Brass, D. J. (2010). Organizational social network research: Core ideas and key debates. *Academy of Management Annals*, **4**(1), 317–357.

Kilduff, M., Crossland, C., Tsai, W. & Bowers, M. T. (2016). Magnification and correction of the acolyte effect: Initial benefits and ex post settling up in NFL coaching careers. *Academy of Management Journal*, **59**(1), 352–375.

Kilduff, M., Crossland, C., Tsai, W. & Krackhardt, D. (2008). Organizational network perceptions versus reality: A small world after all? *Organizational Behavior and Human Decision Processes*, **107**(1), 15–28.

Kilduff, M. & Krackhardt, D. (1994). Bringing the individual back in: A structural analysis of the internal market for reputation in organizations. *Academy of Management Journal*, **37**(1), 87–108.

Kilduff, M. & Lee, J. W. (2020). The integration of people and networks. *Annual Review of Organizational Psychology and Organizational Behavior*, **7**(1), 155–179.

Kilduff, M. & Oh, H. (2006). Deconstructing diffusion: An ethnostatistical examination of medical innovation network data reanalyses. *Organizational Research Methods*, **9**(4), 432–455.

Kilduff, M. & Tsai, W. (2003). *Social Networks and Organizations*. London: Sage.

Kilduff, M., Tsai, W. & Hanke, R. (2006). A paradigm too far? A dynamic stability reconsideration of the social network research program. *Academy of Management Review*, **31**(4), 1031–1048.

Kim, T. Y., Oh, H. & Swaminathan, A. (2006). Framing interorganizational network change: A network inertia perspective. *Academy of Management Review*, **31**(3), 704–720.

Klein, K. J., Lim, B. C., Saltz, J. L. & Mayer, D. M. (2004). How do they get there? An examination of the antecedents of centrality in team networks. *Academy of Management Journal*, **47**(6), 952–963.

Kleinbaum, A. M., Jordan, A. H. & Audia, P. G. (2015). An altercentric perspective on the origins of brokerage in social networks: How perceived empathy moderates the self-monitoring effect. *Organization Science*, **26** (4), 1226–1242.

Kleinbaum, A. M., Stuart, T. E. & Tushman, M. L. (2013). Discretion within constraint: Homophily and structure in a formal organization. *Organization Science*, **24**(5), 1316–1336.

Korte, C. & Milgram, S. (1970). Acquaintance networks between racial groups: Application of the small world method. *Journal of Personality and Social Psychology*, **15**(2), 101–108.

Krackhardt, D. (1987). Cognitive social structures. *Social Networks*, **9**(2), 109–134.

(1988). Predicting with networks: Non-parametric multiple regression analysis of dyadic data. *Social Networks*, **10**(4), 359–381.

(1990). Assessing the political landscape: Structure, cognition, and power in organizations. *Administrative Science Quarterly*, **35**(2), 342–369.

(1992). The strength of strong ties: The importance of philos in organizations. In N. Nohria & R. Eccles, eds., *Networks and Organizations: Structure, Form and Action*. Boston, MA: Harvard Business School Press, pp. 216–239.

(1998). Simmelian ties: Super, strong and sticky. In R. Kramer and M. Neale, eds., *Power and Influence in Organizations*. Thousand Oaks, CA: Sage, pp. 21–38.

(1999). The ties that torture: Simmelian tie analysis in organizations. *Research in the Sociology of Organizations*, **16**, 183–210.

Krackhardt, D. & Hanson, J. R. (1993). Informal networks: The company behind the chart. *Harvard Business Review*, **71**(4), 104–111.

Krackhardt, D. & Kilduff, M. (1999). Whether close or far: Social distance effects on perceived balance in friendship networks. *Journal of Personality and Social Psychology*, **76**(5), 770–782.

(2002). Structure, culture and Simmelian ties in entrepreneurial firms. *Social Networks*, **24**(3), 279–290.

Krackhardt, D. & Porter, L. W. (1986). The snowball effect: Turnover embedded in communication networks. *Journal of Applied Psychology*, **71**(1), 50–55.

Krackhardt, D. & Stern, R. (1988). Informal networks and organizational crises: An experimental simulation. *Social Psychology Quarterly*, **51**(2), 123–140.

Krivitsky, P. N. & Handcock, M. S. (2014). A separable model for dynamic networks. *Journal of the Royal Statistical Society: Series B (Statistical Methodology)*, **76**(1), 29–46.

Kumbasar, E., Romney, A. K. & Batchelder, W. H. (1994). Systematic biases in social perception. *American Journal of Sociology*, **100**(2), 477–505.

Kwon, S. W., Rondi, E., Levin, D. Z., De Massis, A. & Brass, D. J. (2020). Network brokerage: An integrative review and future research agenda. *Journal of Management*, **46**(6), 1092–1120.

Labianca, G. & Brass, D. J. (2006). Exploring the social ledger: Negative relationships and negative asymmetry in social networks in organizations. *Academy of Management Review*, **31**(3), 596–614.

Labianca, G., Brass, D. J. & Gray, B. (1998). Social networks and perceptions of intergroup conflict: The role of negative relationships and third parties. *Academy of Management Journal*, **41**(1), 55–67.

Labianca, G., Fairbank, J. F., Thomas, J. B., Gioia, D. A. & Umphress, E. E. (2001). Emulation in academia: Balancing structure and identity. *Organization Science*, **12**(3), 312–330.

Lakatos, I. (1970). Falsification and the methodology of scientific research programmes. In I. Lakatos & A. Musgrave, eds., *Criticism and the Growth of Knowledge*. Cambridge: Cambridge University Press, pp. 91–196.

Landis, B., Kilduff, M., Menges, J. I. & Kilduff, G. J. (2018). The paradox of agency: Feeling powerful reduces brokerage opportunity recognition yet increases willingness to broker. *Journal of Applied Psychology*, **103**(8), 929–938.

Laudan, L. (1977). *Progress and Its Problems: Towards a Theory of Scientific Growth*. London: Routledge & Kegan Paul.

Laursen, K., Masciarelli, F. & Prencipe, A. (2012). Regions matter: How localized social capital affects innovation and external knowledge acquisition. *Organization Science*, **23**(1), 177–193.

Lazega, E. & Pattison, P. E. (1999). Multiplexity, generalized exchange and cooperation in organizations: A case study. *Social Networks*, **21**(1), 67–90.

Lee, S. H., Kim, P. J., Ahn, Y. Y. & Jeong, H. (2010). Googling social interactions: Web search engine based social network construction. *Plos One*, **5**(7), e11233.

Levin, D. Z., Walter, J. & Murnighan, J. K. (2011). Dormant ties: The value of reconnecting. *Organization Science*, **22**(4), 923–939.

Lewin, K. (1936). *Principles of Topological Psychology*. New York: McGraw-Hill.

Lin, N. (2001). *Social Capital: A Theory of Social Structure and Action*. Cambridge: Cambridge University Press.

Lin, N., Ensel, W. & Vaughn, J. (1981). Social resources and strength of ties: Structural factors in occupational status attainment. *American Sociological Review*, **46**(4), 393–405.

Lomi, A., Lusher, D., Pattison, P. E. & Robins, G. (2014). The focused organization of advice relations: A study in boundary crossing. *Organization Science*, **25**(2), 438–457.

Lorrain, F. & White, H. C. (1971). Structural equivalence of individuals in social networks. *Journal of Mathematical Sociology*, **1**(1), 49–80.

Luce, R. D. & Perry, A. D. (1949). A method of matrix analysis of group structure. *Psychometrika*, **14**, 95–116.

Luk, C. L., Yau, O. H., Sin, L. Y., Tse, A. C., Chow, R. P. & Lee, J. S. (2008). The effects of social capital and organizational innovativeness in different institutional contexts. *Journal of International Business Studies*, **39**(4), 589–612.

Luo, Y. (2007). An integrated anti-opportunism system in international exchange. *Journal of International Business Studies*, **38**(6), 855–877.

Marsden, P. V. (2011). Survey methods for network data. In J. Scott & P. J. Carrington, eds., *Sage Handbook of Social Network Analysis*. London: Sage.

Marsden, P. V. & Campbell, K. E. (1984). Measuring tie strength. *Social Forces*, **63**(2), 482–501.

(2012). Reflections on conceptualizing and measuring tie strength. *Social Forces*, **91**(1), 17–23.

Mayhew, B. H. (1980). Structuralism versus individualism: Part 1, shadowboxing in the dark. *Social Forces*, **59**(2), 335–375.

McPherson, J. M., Smith-Lovin, L. & Brashears, M. E. (2006). Social isolation in America: Changes in core discussion networks over two decades. *American Sociological Review*, **71**(3), 353–375.

Mehra, A., Kilduff, M. & Brass, D. J. (1998). At the margins: A distinctiveness approach to the social identity and social networks of underrepresented groups. *Academy of Management Journal*, **41**(4), 441–452.

(2001). The social networks of high and low self-monitors: Implications for workplace performance. *Administrative Science Quarterly,* **46**(1), 121–146.

Mehra, A., Dixon, A. L., Brass, D. J. & Robertson, B. (2006). The social network ties of group leaders: Implications for group performance and leader reputation. *Organization Science,* **17**(1), 64–79.

Mehra, A., Borgatti, S. P., Soltis, S., Floyd, T., Halgin, D. S., Ofem, B. & Lopez-Kidwell, V. (2014). Imaginary worlds: Using visual network scales to capture perceptions of social networks. *Research in the Sociology of Organizations,* **40**, 315–336.

Menges, J. I. & Kilduff, M. (2015). Group emotions: Cutting the Gordian knots concerning terms, levels of analysis, and processes. *Academy of Management Annals,* **9**(1), 845–928.

Merton, R. K. (1968). *Social Theory and Social Structure.* New York: Free Press.

Meyer, A. D. (1982). Adapting to environmental jolts. *Administrative Science Quarterly,* **27**(4), 515–537.

Milgram, S. (1967). The small world problem. *Psychology Today,* **1**(1), 61–67.

Mizruchi, M. S., Stearns, L. B. & Fleischer, A. (2011). Getting a bonus: Social networks, performance, and reward among commercial bankers. *Organization Science,* **22**(1), 42–59.

Mollica, K. A., Gray, B. & Trevino, L. K. (2003). Racial homophily and its persistence in newcomers' social networks. *Organization Science,* **14**(2), 123–136.

Montgomery, J. D. (1992). Job search and network composition: Implications of the strength-of-weak-tie hypothesis. *American Sociological Review,* **57** (5), 586–596.

Moody, J., McFarland, D. & Bender-deMoll, S. (2005). Dynamic network visualization. *American Journal of Sociology,* **110**(4), 1206–1241.

Moore, M. L. & Westley, F. (2011). Surmountable chasms: Networks and social innovation for resilient systems. *Ecology and Society,* **16**(1), 5.

Moreno, J. L. (1934). *Who Shall Survive? A New Approach to the Problem of Human Interrelations.* Washington, DC: Nervous and Mental Disease Publishing.

Mund, M. & Neyer, F. J. (2014). Treating personality-relationship transactions with respect: Narrow facets, advanced models, and extended time frames. *Journal of Personality and Social Psychology,* **107**(2), 352–368.

Nahapiet, J. & Ghoshal, S. (1998). Social capital, intellectual capital, and the organization advantage. *Academy of Management Review,* **23**(2), 242–266.

Nambisan, S. & Sawhney, M. (2011). Orchestration processes in network-centric innovation: Evidence from the field. *Academy of Management Perspectives,* **25**(3), 40–57.

Nelson, R. E. (1988). Social network analysis as intervention tool: Examples from the field. *Group & Organization Studies*, **13**(1), 39–58.

Newcomb, T. M. (1961). *The Acquaintance Process*. New York: Holt & Rinehart.

Newman, M. E. (2002). Assortative mixing in networks. *Physical Review Letters*, **89**(20), 208701-1–208701-4.

Nicolaou, N. & Kilduff, M. (2022). Empowerment mitigates gender differences in tertius iungens brokering. *Organization Science*. In press.

Obstfeld, D. (2005). Social networks, the *tertius iungens* orientation, and involvement in innovation. *Administrative Science Quarterly*, **50**(1), 100–130.

Obstfeld, D., Borgatti, S. P. & Davis, J. (2014). Brokerage as a process: Decoupling third party action from social network structure. *Contemporary Perspectives on Organizational Social Networks*, **40**, 135–159.

Ogle, D. L., Tenkasi, R. R. V. & Brock, W. B. B. (2020). The social media presence of organization development: A social network analysis using big data. *Research in Organizational Change and Development*, **28**, 1–41.

Oh, H. & Kilduff, M. (2008). The ripple effect of personality on social structure: Self-monitoring origins of network brokerage. *Journal of Applied Psychology*, **93**(5), 1155–1164.

Oh, W. & Jeon, S. (2007). Membership herding and network stability in the open source community: The Ising perspective. *Management Science*, **53**(7), 1086–1101.

O'Mahony, S. & Ferraro, F. (2007). The emergence of governance in an open source community. *Academy of Management Journal*, **50**(5), 1079–1106.

Operti, E., Lampronti, S. Y. & Sgourev, S. V. (2020). Hold your horses: Temporal multiplexity and conflict moderation in the Palio di Siena (1743–2010). *Organization Science*, **31**(1), 85–102.

Padgett, J. F. & Ansell, C. K. (1993). Robust action and the rise of the Medici, 1400–1434. *American Journal of Sociology*, **98**(6), 1259–1319.

Pastor, J. C., Meindl, J. R. & Mayo, M. C. (2002). A network effects model of charisma attributions. *Academy of Management Journal*, **45**(2), 410–420.

Perry, B. L., Pescosolido, B. A. & Borgatti, S. P. (2018). *Egocentric Network Analysis: Foundations, Methods, and Models*. Cambridge: Cambridge University Press.

Perry-Smith, J. E. (2006). Social yet creative: The role of social relationships in facilitating individual creativity. *Academy of Management Journal*, **49**(1), 85–101.

Perry-Smith, J. E. & Shalley, C. E. (2003). The social side of creativity: A static and dynamic social network perspective. *Academy of Management Review*, **28**(1), 89–106.

Pfeffer, J. & Salancik, G. R. (1978). *The External Control of Organizations: A Resource Dependence Perspective.* New York: Harper.

Pinquart, M. & Duberstein, P. R. (2010). Associations of social networks with cancer mortality: A meta-analysis. *Critical Reviews in Oncology/Hematology,* **75**(2), 122–137.

Podolny, J. M. (2001). Networks as the pipes and prisms of the market. *American Journal of Sociology,* **107**(1), 33–60.

Podolny, J. M. & Baron, J. N. (1997). Resources and relationships: Social networks and mobility in the workplace. *American Sociological Review,* **62**(5), 673–693.

Polanyi, M. (1963). The potential theory of absorption: Authority in science has its uses and its dangers. *Science,* **141**(3585), 1010–1013.

Powell, W. W., Koput, K. W. & Smith-Doerr, L. (1996). Interorganizational collaboration and the locus of innovation: Networks of learning in biotechnology. *Administrative Science Quarterly,* **41**(1), 116–145.

Powell, W. W. (1990). Neither market nor hierarchy: Network forms of organization. *Research in Organizational Behavior,* **12**, 295–336.

Prell, C. (2012). *Social Network Analysis: History, Theory and Methodology.* Los Angeles, CA: Sage.

Quintane, E. & Carnabuci, G. (2016). How do brokers broker? Tertius gaudens, tertius iungens, and the temporality of structural holes. *Organization Science,* **27**(6), 1343–1360.

Raider, H. & Krackhardt, D. J. (2002). Intraorganizational networks. In J. A. C. Baum, ed., *The Blackwell Companion to Organizations.* London: Blackwell, pp. 58–74.

Rajkumar, K., Saint-Jacques, G., Bojinov, I., Brynjolfsson, E. & Aral, S. (2022). A causal test of the strength of weak ties. *Science,* **377**(6612), 1304–1310.

Rank, O. N., Robins, G. L. & Pattison, P. E. (2010). Structural logic of intraorganizational networks. *Organization Science,* **21**(3), 745–764.

Ripley, R. M., Snijders, T. A. B., Boda, Z., Vörös, A. & Preciado, P. (2022). *Manual for SIENA* (Version 1.3.8). Oxford: University of Oxford.

Rivera, M. T., Soderstrom, S. B. & Uzzi, B. (2010). Dynamics of dyads in social networks: Assortative, relational, and proximity mechanisms. *Annual Review of Sociology,* **36**, 91–115.

Robins, G., Pattison, P. & Wang, P. (2009). Closure, connectivity and degree distributions: Exponential random graph (p*) models for directed social networks. *Social Networks,* **31**(2), 105–117.

Robins, G., Pattison, P. & Woolcock, J. (2005). Small and other worlds: Global network structures from local processes. *American Journal of Sociology,* **110**(4), 894–936.

Rodan, S. & Galunic, C. (2004). More than network structure: How knowledge heterogeneity influences managerial performance and innovativeness. *Strategic Management Journal*, **25**(6), 541–562.

Roethlisberger, F. J. & Dickson, W. J. (1939). *Management and the Worker*. Cambridge, MA: Harvard University Press.

Rosenquist, J. N., Fowler, J. H. & Christakis, N. A. (2011). Social network determinants of depression. *Molecular Psychiatry*, **16**(3), 273–281.

Sander, T. H. & Putnam, R. D. (2010). Democracy's past and future: Still bowling alone? The post-9/11 split. *Journal of Democracy*, **21**(1), 9–16.

Sasidharan, S., Santhanam, R., Brass, D. J. & Sambamurthy, V. (2012). The effects of social network structure on enterprise systems success: A longitudinal multilevel analysis. *Information Systems Research*, **23** (3-part-1), 658–678.

Sasovova, Z., Mehra, A., Borgatti, S. P. & Schippers, M. C. (2010). Network churn: The effects of self-monitoring personality on brokerage dynamics. *Administrative Science Quarterly*, **55**(4), 639–670.

Schaefer, D. R., Haas, S. A. & Bishop, N. J. (2012). A dynamic model of US adolescents' smoking and friendship networks. *American Journal of Public Health*, **102**(6), e12–e18.

Schulte, M., Cohen, N. A. & Klein, K. J. (2012). The coevolution of network ties and perceptions of team psychological safety. *Organization Science*, **23**(2), 564–581.

Scott, J. (2000). *Social Network Analysis*, 2nd ed. London: Sage.

Scott, J. & Carrington, P. J. (2011). *The SAGE Handbook of Social Network Analysis*. London: Sage.

Shipilov, A. V. & Gawer, A. (2020). Integrating research on interorganizational networks and ecosystems. *Academy of Management Annals*, **14**(1), 92–121.

Shipilov, A. V., Greve, H. R. & Rowley, T. J. (2010). When do interlocks matter? Institutional logics and the diffusion of multiple corporate governance practices. *Academy of Management Journal*, **53**(4), 846–864.

Shipilov, A., Gulati, R., Kilduff, M., Li, S. & Tsai, W. (2014). Relational pluralism within and between organizations. *Academy of Management Journal*, **57**(2), 449–459.

Siciliano, M. D., Welch, E. W. & Feeney, M. K. (2018). Network exploration and exploitation: Professional network churn and scientific production. *Social Networks*, **52**, 167–179.

Simmel, G. (1950). *The Sociology of Georg Simmel*. New York: Free Press. (1955). *Conflict and the Web of Group-Affiliations*. New York: Free Press.

Smith, E. B., Menon, T. & Thompson, L. (2012). Status differences in the cognitive activation of social networks. *Organization Science*, **23**(1), 67–82.

Smith, K. P. & Christakis, N. A. (2008). Social networks and health. *Annual Review of Sociology*, **34**(1), 405–429.

Snijders, T. A. B. (2001). The statistical evaluation of social network dynamics. In M. Sobel & M. Becker, eds., *Sociological Methodology*. Boston, MA: Basil Blackwell, pp. 361–395.

(2005). Models for longitudinal network data. In P. J. Carrington, J. Scott & S. Wasserman, eds., *Models and Methods in Social Network Analysis*. Oxford: Oxford University Press, pp. 215–247.

Snijders, T. A. B., van de Bunt, G. G. & Steglich, C. E. (2010). Introduction to stochastic actor-based models for network dynamics. *Social Networks*, **32** (1), 44–60.

Snijders, T. A. B., Pattison, P. E., Robins, G. L. & Handcock, M. S. (2006). New specifications for exponential random graph models. *Sociological Methodology*, **36**(1), 99–153.

Soda, G., Tortoriello, M. & Iorio, A. (2018). Harvesting value from brokerage: Individual strategic orientation, structural holes, and performance. *Academy of Management Journal*, **61**(3), 896–918.

Soda, G., Usai, A. & Zaheer, A. (2004). Network memory: The influence of past and current networks on performance. *Academy of Management Journal*, **47**(6), 893–906.

Sosa, M. E. (2011). Where do creative interactions come from? The role of tie content and social networks. *Organization Science*, **22**(1), 1–21.

Sparrowe, R. T. & Liden, R. C. (2005). Two routes to influence: Integrating leader-member exchange and network perspectives. *Administrative Science Quarterly*, **50**(4), 505–535.

Spinney, L. (2022). Are we witnessing the dawn of post-theory science? *Guardian*, January 9. www.theguardian.com/technology/2022/jan/09/are-we-witnessing-the-dawn-of-post-theory-science.

Stovel, K. & Shaw, L. (2012). Brokerage. *Annual Review of Sociology*, **38**(1), 139–158.

Stovel, K., Golub, B. & Milgrom, E. M. M. (2011). Stabilizing brokerage. *Proceedings of the National Academy of Sciences*, **108**(Supplement 4), 21326–21332.

Styles, C., Patterson, P. G. & Ahmed, F. (2008). A relational model of export performance. *Journal of International Business Studies*, **39**(5), 880–900.

Sytch, M. & Tatarynowicz, A. (2014). Friends and foes: The dynamics of dual social structures. *Academy of Management Journal*, **57**(2), 585–613.

Tasselli, S. (2015). Social networks and inter-professional knowledge transfer: The case of healthcare professionals. *Organization Studies*, **36**(7), 841–872.

Tasselli, S. & Kilduff, M. (2018). When brokerage between friendship cliques endangers trust: A personality–network fit perspective. *Academy of Management Journal*, **61**(3), 802–825.

(2021). Network agency. *Academy of Management Annals*, **15**(1), 68–110.

Tasselli, S. & Sancino, A. (2023). Leaders' networking behaviours in a time of crisis: A qualitative study on the frontline against COVID-19. *Journal of Management Studies*, **60**(1), 120–173.

Tasselli, S., Kilduff, M. & Landis, B. (2018). Personality change: Implications for organizational behavior. *Academy of Management Annals*, **12**(2), 467–493.

Tasselli, S., Kilduff, M. & Menges, J. I. (2015). The microfoundations of organizational social networks: A review and an agenda for future research. *Journal of Management*, **41**(5), 1361–1387.

Tasselli, S., Neray, B. & Lomi, A. (2023). A network centrality bias: Central individuals in workplace networks have more supportive coworkers. *Social Networks*, **73**(1), 30–41.

Tasselli, S., Zappa, P. & Lomi, A. (2020). Bridging cultural holes in organizations: The dynamic structure of social networks and organizational vocabularies within and across subunits. *Organization Science*, **31**(5), 1292–1312.

Tichy, N. M., Tushman, M. L. & Fombrun, C. (1979). Social network analysis for organizations. *Academy of Management Review*, **4**(4), 507–519.

Tong, S. T., Van Der Heide, B., Langwell, L. & Walther, J. B. (2008). Too much of a good thing? The relationship between number of friends and interpersonal impressions on Facebook. *Journal of Computer-Mediated Communication*, **13**(3), 531–549.

Tortoriello, M., McEvily, B. & Krackhardt, D. (2015). Being a catalyst of innovation: The role of knowledge diversity and network closure. *Organization Science*, **26**(2), 423–438.

Tortoriello, M., Reagans, R. & McEvily, B. (2012). Bridging the knowledge gap: The influence of strong ties, network cohesion, and network range on the transfer of knowledge between organizational units. *Organization Science*, **23**(4), 1024–1039.

Travers, J. & Milgram, S. (1969). An experimental study of the small world problem. *Sociometry*, **32**(4), 425–443.

Tröster, C., Parker, A., Van Knippenberg, D. & Sahlmüller, B. (2019). The coevolution of social networks and thoughts of quitting. *Academy of Management Journal*, **62**(1), 22–43.

Tsai, W. (2001). Knowledge transfer in intraorganizational networks: Effects of network position and absorptive capacity on business unit innovation and performance. *Academy of Management Journal*, **44**(5), 996–1004.

Tsai, W. & Ghoshal, S. (1998). Social capital and value creation: The role of intrafirm networks. *Academy of Management Journal*, **41**(4), 464–476.

Uzzi, B. (1996). The sources and consequences of embeddedness for the economic performance of organizations: The network effect. *American Sociological Review*, **61**(4), 674–698.

  (1997). Social structure and competition in interfirm networks. *Administrative Science Quarterly*, **42**(1), 37–69.

Uzzi, B. & Spiro J. (2005). Collaboration and creativity: The small world problem. *American Journal of Sociology*, **111**(2), 447–504.

Valente, T. W. (2012). Network interventions. *Science*, **337**(6090), 49–53.

Valente, T. W. & Foreman, R. K. (1998). Integration and radiality: Measuring the extent of an individual's connectedness and reachability in a network. *Social Networks*, **20**(1), 89–109.

Vedres, B. & Stark, D. (2010). Structural folds: Generative disruption in overlapping groups. *American Journal of Sociology*, **115**(4), 1150–1190.

Venkataramani, V. & Dalal, R. S. (2007). Who helps and harms whom? Relational antecedents of interpersonal helping and harming in organizations. *Journal of Applied Psychology*, **92**(4), 952–966.

Venkataramani, V., Zhou, L., Wang, M., Liao, H. & Shi, J. (2016). Social networks and employee voice: The influence of team members' and team leaders' social network positions on employee voice. *Organizational Behavior and Human Decision Processes*, **132**(1), 37–48.

Von Hippel, E. (1994). Sticky information and the locus of problem solving: Implications for innovation. *Management Science*, **40**(4), 429–439.

Wang, C., Rodan, S., Fruin, M. & Xu, X. (2014). Knowledge networks, collaboration networks, and exploratory innovation. *Academy of Management Journal*, **57**(2), 484–514.

Wang, P. (2013). Exponential random graph model extensions: Models for multiple networks and bipartite networks. In D. Lusher, J. Koskinen & G. Robins, eds., *Exponential Random Graph Models for Social Networks: Theory, Methods, and Applications*. New York: Cambridge University Press, pp. 115–129.

Wang, P., Robins, G., Pattison, P. & Lazega, E. (2013). Exponential random graph models for multilevel networks. *Social Network*, **35**(1), 96–115.

Wasserman, S. & Faust, K. (1994). *Social Network Analysis: Methods and Applications*. Cambridge: Cambridge University Press.

Watts, D. J. (1999). Networks, dynamics, and the small-world phenomenon. *American Journal of Sociology*, **105**(2), 493–527.

Watts, D. J. & Strogatz, S. H. (1998). Collective dynamics of "small-world" networks. *Nature*, **393**(6684), 440–442.

Webb, E. J., Campbell, D. T., Schwartz, R. D. & Sechrest, L. (1999). *Unobtrusive Measures*. London: Sage.

Weeks, M. R., Scott, C., Borgatti, S. P., Radda, K. & Schensul, J. J. (2002). Social networks of drug users in high-risk sites: Finding the connections. *AIDS and Behavior*, **6**(2), 193–206.

Wellman, B. (1979). The community question. *American Journal of Sociology*, **84**(5), 1201–1231.

  (1988). Structural analysis: From method and metaphor to theory and substance. In B. Wellman & S. D. Berkowitz, eds., *Social Structures: A Network Approach*. Cambridge: Cambridge University Press, pp. 19–61.

Wellman, B. & Berkowitz, S. D. (1988). *Social Structures: A Network Approach*. Cambridge: Cambridge University Press.

White, H. C., Boorman, S. A. & Breiger, R. L. (1976). Social structures from multiple networks: Blockmodels of roles and positions. *American Journal of Sociology*, **81**(4), 730–779.

Whyte, W. F. (1943). *Street Corner Society: The Social Structure of an Italian Slum*. Chicago, IL: University of Chicago Press.

Yakubovich, V. (2005). Weak ties, information, and influence: How workers find jobs in a local Russian labor market. *American Sociological Review*, **70**(3), 408–421.

Young, A. & Hopkins, C. (2015). Semi-automated Processing of Interconnected Dyads using Entity Resolution (SPIDER). National Institutes of Health, Grant #1R43MH106361.

Zachary, W. W. (1977). An information flow model for conflict and fission in small groups. *Journal of Anthropological Research*, **33**(4), 452–473.

Zagenczyk, T. J., Powell, E. E. & Scott, K. L. (2020). How exhausting!? Emotion crossover in organizational social networks. *Journal of Management Studies*, **57**(8), 1589–1609.

Zagenczyk, T. J., Scott, K. D., Gibney, R., Murrell, A. J. & Thatcher, J. B. (2010). Social influence and perceived organizational support: A social networks analysis. *Organizational Behavior and Human Decision Processes*, **111**(2), 127–138.

Zheng, X., Zhao, H. H., Liu, X. & Li, N. (2019). Network reconfiguration: The implications of recognizing top performers in teams. *Journal of Occupational and Organizational Psychology*, **92**(4), 825–847.

Zhou, K. Z., Poppo, L. & Yang, Z. (2008). Relational ties or customized contracts? An examination of alternative governance choices in China. *Journal of International Business Studies*, **39**(3), 526–534.

Zuckerman, E. W. (1999). The categorical imperative: Securities analysts and the illegitimacy discount. *American Journal of Sociology*, **104**(5), 1398–1438.

Cambridge Elements ☰

Organization Theory

Nelson Phillips
UC Santa Barbara

Nelson Phillips is the Abu Dhabi Chamber Professor of Strategy and Innovation at Imperial College London. His research interests include organization theory, technology strategy, innovation, and entrepreneurship, often studied from an institutional theory perspective.

Royston Greenwood
University of Alberta

Royston Greenwood is the Telus Professor of Strategic Management at the University of Alberta, a visiting professor at the University of Cambridge, and a visiting professor at the University of Edinburgh. His research interests include organizational change and professional misconduct.

About the Series

Organization theory covers many different approaches to understanding organizations. Its focus is on what constitutes the how and why of organizations and organizing, bringing understanding of organizations in a holistic way. The purpose of Elements in Organization Theory is to systematize and contribute to our understanding of organizations.

Cambridge Elements ⹀

Organization Theory

Elements in the Series

Printed in the United States
by Baker & Taylor Publisher Services

Printed in the United States
by Baker & Taylor Publisher Services